Power Animals

Unlocking the Mystical Wisdom of Totem Spirits through Shamanic Journeying, Dream Interpretation, and Intuitive Connections

Free Bonus from Silvia Hill available for limited time

Hi Spirituality Lovers!

My name is Silvia Hill, and first off, I want to THANK YOU for reading my book.

Now you have a chance to join my exclusive spirituality email list so you can get the ebooks below for free as well as the potential to get more spirituality ebooks for free! Simply click the link below to join.

P.S. Remember that it's 100% free to join the list.

~~$27~~ FREE BONUSES

🖐 9 Types of Spirit Guides and How to Connect to Them

🖐 How to Develop Your Intuition: 7 Secrets for Psychic Development and Tarot Reading

🖐 Tarot Reading Secrets for Love, Career, and General Messages

Access your free bonuses here
https://livetolearn.lpages.co/power-animals-paperback/

Table of Contents

Introduction

It's truly fascinating how animals are present in every part of our lives and daily consciousness in one form or another. You can see them physically, like the beautiful birds chirping outside your window or the spiders building webs in the corners of your rooms. Or you could think of it in another way. These animals also manifest symbolically, like the totems of wolves, tortoises, raccoons, and hawks that may sit on your desk or the poster of a beautiful butterfly adorning your wall.

This close bond you share with the animal kingdom can be seen in so many ways. Even in the city, you can see so many animals, whether it's pigeons, squirrels, cats, or even small rats scuttling about. If you stroll through a forest, you might find rabbits darting around or wild turkeys looking for food. Every day, pets like dogs, cats, goldfish, and hamsters serve as reminders of this connection.

Even sports teams and organizations adopt animal names, like the Philadelphia Eagles or Seattle Seahawks, and groups like the Lion's Club or the Loyal Order of Moose. Animals are a common theme in fairy tales, talking effortlessly with humans. The bottom line is that animals are a huge part of your life that cannot be ignored, and for good reason. Without animals, this would stop functioning, literally!

In addition to their obvious importance in this world, they also serve a latent function. All animals hold important teachings for you. For instance, ants showcase the power of community, while lions highlight leadership values. There's such a wide variety of wisdom in the animal world, but you can connect with specific animals you feel drawn to and develop a special connection with them. These are called your power animals, sacred companions that you can call upon to help you on your healing journey.

The lessons they bring and the gifts they share have a deep meaning for you. These animals can be thought of as your reflection. The qualities you observe in your power animal, the emotions they stir up, the good and the bad, are all part of you, too. If they weren't, you wouldn't be able to connect with them in the first place. Your power animals are like your personal guides, and they can help you heal. This book will guide you through discovering your power animals and help you learn about the different shamanic techniques to interpret the messages conveyed by one's power animal.

Chapter 1: What Is a Power Animal?

People always seek guidance and answers to many of life's complicated questions. They wish life came with a manual or an answer key they can look at whenever they are struggling with a decision. However, life isn't that simple. Human beings are meant to make mistakes and go on multiple journeys of self-discovery. It is the only way you will learn. So, does that mean life will never lend you a helping hand?

Perhaps one of the most comforting thoughts is that you are never truly alone. There are many invisible forces around you willing to offer you guidance. They are probably sending you signs right now or opening your eyes to certain truths, but you don't notice them. People are accustomed to seeing random occurrences as coincidences rather than believing something or someone is looking out for them.

The spirit realm is vast and complex, with many secrets the human mind doesn't always comprehend. There are many invisible forces in that realm. You should never fear or avoid them, for they are allies and constantly try to help you. Some of these forces are called power animals.

This chapter introduces you to power animals, their role in Shamanism, and how you can connect with them.

What Is a Power Animal?

Power animals are spirit guides that are connected to your spiritual energy. They often appear to you in dreams, meditation, visions, or shamanic journeys. In some cases, they can appear in the real world in their physical form. For instance, if your power animal is an owl, you will keep seeing it in random places. They can be reptiles, insects, birds, or mammals. Power animals can also be mythical creatures like dragons or unicorns, but they won't appear in a physical state since they don't exist in real life. They often become guides to the people who believe in their existence.

Power animals are spirit guides that are connected to your spiritual energy.
https://unsplash.com/photos/BpH-upRlCs

However, they aren't real animals but share the same qualities as those they represent. They draw their power from their wild and instinctual nature. So, it is more likely a power animal will be a lion or a fox than your pet dog or the stray cat you feed in your neighborhood. Although many people wish their pets could be power animals, this is highly unlikely. Domesticated animals haven't spent time in the wild and don't have the same connection to nature as bears, lions, elephants, etc.

So, they don't have what it takes to be power animals.

A power animal gets its abilities and strengths from an entire species, not just one animal. For instance, if your power animal is a tiger, the spirit guide won't represent one tiger but its entire species. If it's a shark, you will love all species of shark and will develop an appreciation for and interest in all sea creatures.

Your power animal will use the love and compassion you have for its species to empower and heal you and the people in your life.

You shouldn't fear your animal because they intend to help and guide you to deal with changes and obstacles. They are trustworthy spirits with rare wisdom and insight, and you can always turn to them for answers or guidance. They are in tune with nature and the physical and spirit worlds, so they can see the things you don't and better understand the universe. Power animals are teachers and can transform your life. If you work with them, they will expand your horizons and spiritual capacities so you can see things differently.

Every person has a power animal. You can discover yours by opening yourself to the idea. Your soul, mind, and heart need to believe that these spirits exist and that you can reach out to them. Sometimes, your power animal will initiate communication with you. For instance, if you keep seeing a bear in your dreams, it could be your power animal revealing their identity to you.

If there is an animal that you usually gravitate toward, it is probably your power animal. Dr. Steven Farmer, a shamanic healer and author of many books about spirit and power animals, said that one of his readers sent him a message asking if he could help her discover her power animal. She also mentioned how hawks have appeared multiple times throughout her life, and she was wondering if this was her power animal.

Dr. Steven replied that what she felt in her gut was correct and the hawk was indeed her power animal.

Each person has one or more from the day they are born. Although they are always in your life, they keep changing to fulfill different needs in every spiritual path you take.

A power animal won't stay with you forever. It comes into your life for a reason, and once it fulfills its purpose, it leaves. You shouldn't feel sad or take their departure personally. Power animals come and go in and out of your life. Rest assured that when one leaves, another takes its place right away to guide you through a new stage of your life.

The power animal that comes into your life will represent your current needs. For instance, if you have been promoted to a management position, a lion power animal will show up to raise your self-esteem and provide you with leadership skills. If you are experiencing big changes, your power animal can be a snake that will encourage you to grow and transform.

Your power animal will reflect your main characteristics. For instance, if you are a confident person who leads rather than follows, your power animal can be a cougar.

Your relationship with your power animal is special, so nurture and care for it. If you give it the attention it deserves, it will be in your life for a long time and happily offer guidance whenever you call on it.

Power Animals vs. Spirit Animals vs. Totem Animals

There are many entities in the spirit world. Many of them take the form of animals like power animals, spirit animals, and totem animals. While it can be easy to confuse the three, they are not the same.

Spirit Animals

Spirit animals are energies or entities that live in the spirit realm but can cross to the physical world to guide people through different phases of their lives.
https://pixabay.com/illustrations/wolf-spirit-animal-space-soul-7746782/

Spirit animals are energies or entities that live in the spirit realm but can cross to the physical world to guide people through different phases of their lives. Your relationship with your spirit animal is deep and personal, but it can change when you experience growth or transformation. The spirit animal that comes into your life will answer the questions you have right now.

If you call on your spirit animal for guidance, it will often appear to you to nudge you in the right direction. For instance, you want to change your career but are afraid to take this step. Your spirit animal can appear to you as a butterfly to signal that change is always beautiful and not to be feared.

A spirit animal will reveal itself to you by appearing in dreams, meditations, images in advertisements, TV, online, psychic impressions, and many other methods.

So far, they sound exactly like power animals, right? However, there are a few subtle differences. Unlike power animals, spirit animals don't share any of your personality traits. Their messages are also different. Spirit animals offer guidance for specific situations or to overcome certain challenges. For instance, your spirit animal can appear when you struggle to get out of an abusive relationship. Power animals, conversely, will guide you by revealing your true potential and inspire you to reflect on your inner strengths to achieve empowerment and self-realization.

Spirit animals will leave after they finish their job and will only reappear when you need them again. However, power animals never leave you. They can change, but you will always have one by your side.

Totem Animals

Individual totemism is when a person believes that an object from nature or an animal can give them power.
Bernard Spragg. NZ from Christchurch, New Zealand, CC0, via Wikimedia Commons:
https://commons.wikimedia.org/wiki/File:Totem_poles._Vancouver._(9625452417).jpg

There are two types of totem animals: one is related to individuals, while the other is associated with groups. Individual totemism is when a person believes that an object from nature or an animal can give them power. It becomes a part of you through a bond that happens before birth.

Group totemism describes animals, natural phenomena, or plants representing a tribe, clan, or family. They are usually associated with their ancestors and can offer guidance and protection. These groups believe their totems have magical powers and can even shapeshift into human beings.

Many cultures believe in totem animals, such as Native Americans, and they assign different qualities to them. For instance, they consider elephants as symbols of harmony, unity, strength, and wisdom.

Like power animals, totems will stay in your life permanently and won't disappear like spirit animals. However, unlike power animals, totem animals are symbols associated with a group's heritage passed down from generation to generation.

Totems offer guidance differently from both power and spirit animals. They focus on a group's common beliefs, values, and experiences. They represent the identity and bond within families and tribes. Spirit animals focus on the person's spiritual path, while power animals focus on the individual personal traits.

Power Animals in Shamanism

Shamans believe that everything in life has wisdom and power, so they associate power animal guides with these two traits. These guides play a big role in shamanic practice. They act as helpful spirits that empower shamans and strengthen their abilities so they can undertake any venture.

In Shamanism, every person has a power animal by their side throughout their life's journey. They believe these animals are similar to guardian angels as they offer protection and empowerment and heal them from physical and spiritual ailments. They shield you from negative energy and protect you from dark entities that want to harm you. Your power animal will also imbue you with the wisdom and qualities of its species.

They also believe that power animals connect you to your intuition. Like meditation and yoga, they can make you reach the deepest parts of yourself.

According to Shamanism, people are born with one power animal but encounter many others throughout their lives. Some stay with you for years, while others fulfill their purpose and leave. However, another must come and take its place right away. If it doesn't, and you remain without a power animal, you will lose strength and suffer from misfortune and diseases. In this case, you must seek the help of a shaman to recover your power animal so you can heal.

Shamans consider power animals allies, guides, and protectors on a spiritual journey. During shamanic healing rituals, a shaman becomes something called "The hollow bone" and transforms into a healer who gets power from his animal allies.

Shamans use power animals to heal themselves and others from bad situations like toxic relationships and guide people to find lost objects, overcome obstacles, and achieve their goals.

In Shamanism, any living creature, except humans, plants, and trees, can be power animals - even insects. Shamans claim that they can communicate with animals. Many have mentioned that they can shapeshift into animals by practicing certain rituals that involve dancing, singing, and drumming.

Drumming is one of the most popular methods among shamans for connecting with power animals. During this ceremony, the power animal that reaches out to you will be the one you need to continue your life's journey.

Shamans believe a power animal chooses the person they want to connect with and will reveal itself to you at the right time. However, sometimes their messages or symbols can be subtle, so keep your eyes open to notice the signs.

Connecting with Your Power Animal

You can connect with your power animal to seek their wisdom and guidance in different ways. Remember, your power animal is out there and has been around for years. All you need to do to find them is to initiate communication.

Shamanic Journeying

Shamanic journeying is an ancient ritual and one of the most popular and interesting methods to find your power animal. During this ritual, a shaman will put you in a trance state to take you on a spiritual journey using drums. You will find yourself in a different reality beyond time and space, seeing and feeling things on a deeper and higher level. On this journey, your power animal will reveal itself to you. However, it will take time, and you'll need to keep performing this ritual a few times before you get real results.

Meditation

Meditation is another powerful technique used to connect with your power animal. Many meditation techniques will be discussed later in the book, and you can practice them daily to find your power animal. During meditation, you will learn to relax, calm your mind, and focus on one thought, reaching out to your power animal. Once you establish a connection, you can seek its wisdom, ask it anything, or request its protection or guidance.

Meditation is another powerful technique used to connect with your power animal.
https://pixabay.com/illustrations/meditation-spiritual-yoga-1384758/

Dreams

As you begin your journey to find your power guide, it can reveal its identity through dreams. It is one of the easiest methods they use to reach out to their humans. In the dream world, anything is possible, and there isn't any room for disbelief. They will also be in control and can create any scenario they choose to send you a message. Pay attention to your dreams and understand that nothing you see is random. Your power animal will either reveal itself to you in its true form or send you symbols or clues to decipher and uncover its identity.

Intuitive Experiences

Do you know your power animal? Don't answer right away. Take a few minutes and think. On some level, you may feel which animal is your power spirit guide. You may have the answer in your gut or intuition. Perhaps you have noticed signs that got your attention, or the animal keeps appearing to you in strange places that you believe can't be coincidences. Or maybe you just know. Trust your intuition because it will never lead you astray.

Encounters in Nature

This technique is very simple and straightforward. You can see your power animal in physical form in nature. Remember, what you'll see isn't your real power animal but a symbol of it.

So, spend time in nature, observe the animals, and see if one gets your attention.

Approaching Your Power Animals

What should you do when you find your power animal? How do you approach them? Shamans believe you should appreciate your power animal and treat it with humility and respect. Whenever you ask for a favor, you should always express your gratitude. Simply say thank you after making a request or when they offer you guidance.

When a friend, co-worker, or even a stranger does you a favor, you always say "Thank you," right? This is how you develop healthy relationships with the people in your life. Similarly, when you show your spirit animal that you are grateful for its support, it will strengthen your bond, and your spirit animal will feel appreciated and happy to help you every time.

In shamanic cultures, honoring power animals is a vital part of the rituals. Some cultures don't value or respect animals for the gifts they constantly give. Have you ever seen someone appreciate a cow for its milk?

Shamans value animals highly and understand they can't practice their shamanic work without their power spirits. They understand that these spirits give so much and require so little in return.

You can honor your power animal by getting an object that symbolizes it and placing it where you can always see it. For instance, if your spirit animal is a fox, you can get one tattooed on your body, wear it as a piece of jewelry with a fox pendant, or buy a fox statue and put it on your desk at work or in your living room.

What to Expect from This Book?

In the coming chapters, you will learn in detail different methods to communicate with power animals. The book sheds light on the spiritual and practical significance of power animals within indigenous cultures and their diverse belief systems and practices.

Many animals can be your power spirit guides. You will learn the most common ones and their qualities, attributes, symbolism, and significance.

One of the book's most interesting and significant parts is discovering how to call on your power animal. You will learn various techniques that you can use to identify it and how to connect with its qualities and attributes once you develop a connection.

The book introduces the practice of shamanic journeying and dreams as effective means of meeting and communicating with power animals. There are two separate chapters in the book focusing on each method. You will learn about the different types of shamanic journeys and their purpose and discover the three shamanic worlds.

Since your power animal may not appear in its true form in your dream, the book introduces common animal symbols and their potential interpretations so you can figure out the clues it is sending you.

You can also invite your power animal to your dreams. This requires certain rituals like affirmations or visualization techniques. You will also discover how to control your dreams by learning techniques for achieving lucid dreaming.

You will also learn how to strengthen your bond with your power animal and get over specific challenges you may encounter when working with it.

The book also discusses various healing techniques for physical, emotional, mental, and spiritual imbalances. The last chapter includes methods you can use to apply the guidance and teachings of power animals in your daily life.

Your power animal has always been with you. It has never left your side since you took your first breath. Its only purpose is to guide and help you. Open your heart, eyes, and mind because deep down, you know who your power spirit guide is. If your gut feeling isn't giving you an answer, keep reading to discover how to communicate and have a relationship with your power animal.

Chapter 2: Animals in Indigenous Culture

The oldest spiritual systems on the planet are deeply connected to nature. Common descriptions of a divine life force connecting all are found in most ancient cultures. Viewing the divine separated from nature is a relatively new concept that would have been confusingly foreign to humanity's distant ancestry. Shamanic traditions keep the sacredness of animals alive with mythology, symbolism, and ecstatic visionary experiences. People learned through observation before books and countless other ways of transmitting lessons came along. Their first teacher was the living environment they interacted with daily for survival. In the modern age, there is a disconnect from the life that sustains the world, so nature does not get deified in the same way as it does in ancient traditions.

Through observing how animals lived and connecting with them in the spiritual realm through dreams and trance experiences, people discovered how the connection with animals is beyond the physical. Indigenous practices seek to embody the admirable qualities of animals observed in nature and accessed through Shamanic exploration. Therefore, complex mythology and symbology have been birthed globally by ancient cultures. There are many common archetypes and symbolic expressions of animals connecting cultures worldwide that lived thousands of miles and centuries apart. Exploring the common narratives and beliefs about animals and their spiritual significance can reveal much about the power that can be used by communing with animals in the spirit world.

Animal Deities

Sekhmet was a lioness deity representing war and the destruction of enemies.
Mary Harrsch, CC BY-SA 4.0 <https://creativecommons.org/licenses/by-sa/4.0>, via Wikimedia Commons:
https://commons.wikimedia.org/wiki/File:Black_granite_statue_of_the_goddess_Sekhmet_excacvated_at_Ra
messeum_in_Thebes_Egypt_1405-1367_BCE_Late_18th_Dynasty_Penn_Museum_02.jpg

Animals have been worshipped since the dawn of civilization, and we cannot deny the spiritual standing that animals hold in all cultures. In Christian literature, the creation story had a serpent as a central narrative component. Islamic traditions speak of the *Buraq*, a winged, horse-like creature that the Prophet Muhammad rode. In India, many Hindus honor cows as sacred, and many temples are dedicated to deities that have animalistic appearances. Observing animals inspires awe in humans, so it makes sense that people's admiration for animal life is reflected in the mythologies and belief systems many hold dear.

The complex stories of animal deities in indigenous cultures reveal much about how people relate to the natural world. Ancient Egypt is one of the oldest civilizations on Earth. Many consider the region the progenitor of global culture because of its profound impact on Greece, Rome, and the ancient Near East. The ancient Egyptians had several deities with animal features. Sekhmet was a lioness deity representing war and the destruction of enemies. The goddess of war was depicted as a lioness due to how fierce and powerful the animal is.

Furthermore, lionesses do most of the hunting in a pride, so the deity being expressed as the female of the species is a direct parallel. Anubis is another animal deity in ancient Egypt. Anubis is the god of the underworld and is shown as a jackal. The underworld is infinite darkness, so the jackal, known for its great eyesight, is the perfect animal to guide your soul into the void.

Trickster deities in various cultures have often been represented using animal forms. The Marvel cinematic universe has popularized ancient deities like Thor and Loki. In the Norse tradition, Thor was often associated with mountain goats, and Loki was a trickster deity who shapeshifted, often taking the form of the serpent. A parallel can be drawn between Loki as a trickster serpent and the serpent in the Garden of Eden that deceived Adam and Eve. West and Central Africa also have a shapeshifting trickster called Ananzi. The often vengeful deity also appears as a spider. Spiders and snakes live in dark corners, can camouflage well, and are often dangerous. Their hiddenness, coupled with the potential to harm, is why they can often be perceived as deceptive.

Many deities in the ancient world are hybrids between humans and animals. This fusion of human and beast is the artistic depiction of how humans can evolve by adopting animal traits and the intrinsic connection between people and animals. The Greek god Pan is half man and half goat. Pan is the deity of shepherds and the wild. Pan's behavior was often primal and represented the animalistic drive of humans. The animal half of Pan was at the bottom to represent human's animalistic urges as lower. The Egyptian god Heru is also part animal and part human. With Heru, the animal is used to reflect man's higher nature. Heru has the head of a hawk, a bird of prey that flies higher than most birds. The soaring hawk being the head of the god shows people should elevate their minds as high as a hawk's. Furthermore, the hawk sees all from its elevated position, so raising your mind will provide clarity.

Totem and Spirit Animals

A totem can be described as an animal or natural object that holds sacred significance to a particular culture or society. Crafts, statues, talismans, and altars are made to honor the spirits or symbolic representations of ideas depicted as animals. Totems can be assigned according to birth and region but can also be used as a mark of membership to a sacred order. There are collective totems that represent a tribe or a family, as well as totems that connect with individuals. Spirit animals are a subsection of the umbrella term totem. Totems can appear as animals, supernatural entities, and human-animal hybrids.

Many Native American cultures have a strong tradition of constructing totem poles and assigning animal totems to clans or families. Traditionally, clans or families are not permitted to harm, kill, or eat the animal totem that represents them. Your totem animal will guide you through life in both the material and spiritual realms. Totem animals can be compared to Biblical concepts such as angels and the Western traditions of saints. Totem animals have many different meanings depending on region and culture. In some Native American traditions, bears symbolize leadership and strength, birds symbolize a carefree nature, dogs represent the healing of internal wounds, and moles are connected to the spirit of the earth.

Totem animals can be contacted in a variety of ways. Art, crafts, singing, chanting, dancing, and complex rituals are geared toward interacting with these spiritual guides. Southern African Khoisan tribes wore animal skins, feathers, and masks to channel the spirit of the animals. The traditional leader of the ceremony dances for hours around the fire to the hypnotic rhythm of pounding, repetitive drums. The leader, or Shaman, will mimic the movements and mannerisms of the animal. In the nomadic hunter/gatherer days, the Khoisan tribes would do these kinds of rituals that emulate the movements of animals to connect and understand the psychology of the beast more deeply so they could hunt them better. The rituals also helped the tribe embody the favorable characteristics of the animals they honored. In these ancient cultures, even though the meat of animals was consumed, there was respect and reverence in the understanding that animals were giving their lives for the benefit of the tribe.

Animal totems can be worn as jewelry, carved as a standing structure, or etched into the skin with various designs. Body modifications to represent animals are common in Sub-Saharan Africa. The Bali people in Nigeria and the Bondei and Shambaa in Tanzania have scarification practices to carve patterns into the skin to represent the bird ancestors of whom they see themselves as reincarnation. The Moru of South Sudan and the Bobo of Burkina Faso both have scarring practices meant to resemble crocodile skin patterns. Herbal medicine is rubbed into the scars to infect the wound and enhance its prominence. Wearing your skin as an animal Totem is a powerful symbolic representation because the skin is the biggest organ and is the layer of human biology that interacts directly with the world. Furthermore, the pain involved in undergoing the scarification ritual is a rite of passage because one is unlikely to forget such an ordeal, so the importance of the marking is branded on the wearer's mind until death.

Animal Symbology and Mythology

Archeologists once thought humans began pondering their place in the world and their spiritual reality after the advent of agriculture. Researchers theorized agriculture gave humans more free time because they no longer had to hunt constantly. This newly found free time was used to question the existence and develop mythologies that would later become religions. This view is now under question because complex carvings, artwork, and architecture have been discovered in ancient sites in the Americas that are older than the age of agriculture. Humans have likely had a spiritual awareness that long predates civilization or farming. Some of the oldest cave paintings show images of animals, so humans have been closely observing the animal world for decades.

It is easy to see how human interactions with the natural world could cause the formation of complex cosmologies and mythologies. By looking at an anthill in the backyard, there are centuries of wisdom hidden in their behavior. Ants show collaboration and determination, which is admirable. Humans relate more to a story than cold, hard data. Therefore, the formation of mythologies created through interacting with and observing animals is a perfect way to integrate behaviors that can increase well-being. From creation stories to fables and apocalyptic visions, animals play a central role in facilitating the messages set thousands of years into the future.

The position animals play in mythologies can take several forms. Animals can be depicted as adversarial forces or as guides that assist people. This shows the multi-level understanding that primordial people had about how the natural world both benefits and hinders you. Nature creates you, and nature will eventually destroy you. Mythology dwells in this interplay between the natural world's terrifying might and human dependence on Mother Nature as a nurturer. Animals have been described in ways that make them heroic, as well as stories that highlight them as demonic. In one culture, a certain animal may be regarded as powerful, while in another, it can symbolize bad luck.

Animals have been described in ways that make them heroic, as well as stories that highlight them as demonic.

Mythologies do not have to be communicated in long, drawn-out narratives. Some of the most powerful mythologies are spoken in just a few words. For example, in Japan, it is said that a crane lives for one thousand years, while a turtle lives for ten thousand years. In Japan, cranes and turtles are used as symbols of longevity. Turtles have a unique place in global mythology, with the animal often being linked to human origins. In Japan, a turtle held up the place where the immortals dwelled, known locally as Turtle Mountain. Indigenous people call some parts of North and Central America Turtle Island because native mythologies record that the region was formed on the back of a turtle.

The turtle is not the only animal tied into creation mythology. In the Amazon, many Shamanic songs sung during rituals and ceremonies refer to the Amazon River as a sacred anaconda. The Milky Way galaxy is viewed as a cosmic anaconda that is the source of all life on Earth. Just like American and Asian traditions outline the turtle's central role in creation, Amazonian traditions put the anaconda at the center of their creation. In the ancient Near East, dragons were primordial energies that had a hand in the chaotic creation of reality. Dragons, anacondas, and turtles are all reptilian. Reptiles seem to be included in many ancient creation myths. It's interesting to note that the oldest part of the human brain is called the "reptilian brain." In scientific terms, the reptilian brain is not an evolution from reptiles, but most reptiles have a similar brain structure. The reptilian brain deals with our base urges, or the most ancient parts of our biology linked to survival. The indigenous people did not have the modern tools to explore this connection, yet came to similar conclusions using spiritual means and possibly guidance from spirit animals.

Animals in Ritual

Animals have been used in rituals from time immemorial. Animal sacrifice has been common throughout cultures in the world. In Southern Africa, traditional healers get possessed by their ancestors or various spirits during their initiation graduation ceremony. The spirits that possess the healer drink animal blood, so the throat of a goat is slit while the traditional healer drinks from its neck in an ecstatic state. In the Old Testament, there was a system of sacrifice headed by the Levitical priestly order. Specific animals were slaughtered for various festivals or the repentance of sin.

The Israelite practices of the Torah grew out of older traditions in the ancient Near East. Canaanite and Edomite groups used goats as divination tools. A goat was ritually slaughtered, and its liver was removed. The liver was then read by priests in the group to diagnose problems or look into the future. In this way, the animal world has become a catalyst for communing with the spirit world or the invisible influences of reality. The sacrificial narrative of the Old Testament spilled over into Christianity, with Jesus Christ being described as a lamb.

In the Hindu tradition, cows are used in sacred ceremonies. When someone buys a new home or a visitor arrives, a cow may enter the family's yard or even their home. The cow brings in blessings and good fortune. In most parts of India, cows are not slaughtered or eaten. Cows are sometimes used for milk or to work on the farm but will not be killed. Many Hindu sects honor cows as deities and give them the highly respected title of "mother." Cows are decorated elaborately in ceremonies and are treated with the utmost respect. Cow dung is sometimes burned as incense as a way to usher in blessings, as well as a cleansing ritual.

The Benna and Hamer tribes that inhabit the Omo Valley of Ethiopia use bulls as a rite of passage into manhood and a way to get a wife. To be considered a man, you must run across the backs of twelve bulls lined up next to each other. If a man falls when jumping these bulls, it is considered a disgrace to him and his family. A man cannot wed until he has accomplished this difficult feat. Boys practice for months to ensure they do not mess up on the important day when they must prove themselves worthy of being a man. Bulls are used in this way as a gateway into a different part of a man's life.

Shamanic Journeys with Spirit Animals

Many of the rituals previously discussed focus on how animals are used in the physical for spiritual and social reasons. Not much has touched on animals in the spiritual realm. In the Shamanic traditions, the spiritual and natural worlds are not seen as separate but as different elements of the same reality. Just like you cannot see your breath but can detect it in various ways, the spiritual realm can be observed using specialized skills. Shamanic journeys are based on altered states. These states of consciousness that thin the veil between the natural world and the spiritual realm are accessed using herbal mixtures, singing, chanting, and breathing exercises to reach trance states.

In these altered states, Shamans can interact with spirits and energies directly. The Shaman becomes your guide through the uncharted territories you are about to explore. The initiation processes and experience allow the Shaman to know exactly what to do to get you to the desired position for your healing. In these trance spaces, you'll encounter animal spirits. You can meet your animal guides through breath control, chanting, drumming, and herbal medicine. Animal spirits in traditional shamanism provide people with guidance through life issues, as well as physical and psychological healing. People have recorded experiences of meeting light serpents that eat the negative energy out of their bodies and encountering spirit animals that have worked with their lineage for decades.

In Western and Southern African traditions, animal spirits call you to become a traditional healer in dreams or visions. Common animals encountered in these calling experiences are panthers, large serpents, and even human-animal hybrids like mermaids. These animal spirits guide shamans along their journey by revealing secrets of the universe, which aids in providing the knowledge to heal. Shamans do not work like Western doctors, where you go in and tell them your problems. Shamans consult the spirit world, where they get information about you and your spiritual condition. As initiates, legitimate Shamans and traditional healers are well-suited to introduce you to the animal spirits that have been with you for eons. However, by jumping into some of their practices, like meditation or spiritual dance, you can open the same doorways.

Shamanism views animal spirits like elders. Instead of the elders being 70 to 80 years old, these elders have been around for thousands of years, maybe since the foundations of the universe were laid. Some people, especially through a Western Europeanized lens, view these animal spirits as manifestations of the mind more than supernatural beings. Whether these experiences with wise animal spirits are supernatural or psychological phenomena, they still provide deep insights into the human experience and the place people occupy in the universe. Meeting your power animals gives you access to another level of perception that you can use to make beneficial decisions for your life. When humans do not have the answers, animal spirits seem to appear right on cue. Maybe if humanity can let go of the tight grip on the steering wheel of ego, these animal guides and deities can step in to drive the world off the path of destruction, depression, and ecological massacre.

Chapter 3: Power Animals from A to Z

This chapter is about the meaning, symbolism, and inspiration of power animals and is a handy, quick reference guide to find out how each power animal can help you. Start from the beginning, or just flip open and read something randomly. If you see an animal out in the world or dream about one, you can look it up here. Think about your three main power animals and write notes in your journal. Sometimes, you might not know why a certain animal appeals to you or what it's trying to tell you. Just keep listening to what you feel inside.

When you read about a certain animal, do you feel a little pull in your stomach, just below your chest? Do you want to stop reading and learn more about that animal or watch it closely? Trust your gut feeling. Remember, the animals you're drawn to might change depending on the time or day. Your three main power animals are always with you. But sometimes, you might need other animals' help, too. Therefore, you should also learn about the symbolism behind every other animal.

Alligator (Crocodile)

Alligators have strong bodies covered in tough scales and can move quickly in water and on land.
https://unsplash.com/photos/PcS4vRMc7d8

People often think of alligators and crocodiles as tough and aggressive creatures. They have strong bodies covered in tough scales and can move quickly in water and on land. Their powerful jaws and tails can easily catch and defeat their prey. However, even though they seem dangerous, you can learn something valuable from them. Alligators spend a lot of time in the water where they feel at home. They move gracefully through the water, relying on their instincts to survive. You also have instincts deep inside you, like when you react quickly to danger. Just like alligators, you can use these instincts to do great things.

Long ago, the ancient Egyptians admired a god with a crocodile head named Sobek. They liked how strong and protective he was. This idea inspired their leaders to care for their people and land. Alligators defend their territory and young, show you how to set boundaries, care for your home, and protect what's important.

Ant

The learning point from ants is their sense of community, as they live in big groups and help each other out.

https://unsplash.com/photos/CAOZbgPa-7o

When you see a tiny ant by itself, it might not seem like a very "powerful" animal per se, considering that it could easily get hurt. However, there's more to ants than meets the eye. They never live alone, and there are so many of them worldwide. Some ant groups work in teams, building things together and even creating bridges or rafts with their bodies. Ants have been around for a really long time, even when dinosaurs were around.

The learning point from ants is their sense of community, as they live in big groups and help each other out. They also team up with other plants and animals in useful ways. Even though humans often think of ants as pests, like the ones that sting or ruin trees, they actually help in some places. They make the soil better and can control pests naturally.

Plus, animals don't solely exist to be useful to humans. They have their own value and role in the world. This goes for pets, too - you do not really own them. Instead, you share your lives with them. Ants don't care if you understand them or not. They just keep doing their *ant things* - like working, eating, building, exploring, and caring for their nest. This is a good reminder for you to do your part and work together because there is incredible strength in unity.

Bat

As bats thrive in darkness, you can find good things and learn lessons during tough times.
https://unsplash.com/photos/yLSKobI0XYA

Bats live in two worlds: they are grounded creatures that stay deep in caves in the earth, but they can also fly high in the sky using their wings. Some people think bats are connected to evil or death, but if you look closer, you'll see how diverse and crucial they are. They help plants grow by spreading pollen, controlling insects, and doing a lot more to keep nature in balance worldwide.

What's really amazing is that some bats can "see" in the dark by making sounds that bounce back from obstacles and bugs, which helps them navigate to find food and avoid crashing into places. They use their hearts and instincts to guide them, not just their eyes. They, therefore, teach you to listen to your feelings and intuition, even when things seem confusing. When you feel lost or troubled, you can think of bats and remember to trust your inner wisdom and not get distracted by anything.

As bats thrive in darkness, you can find good things and learn lessons during tough times. Bats show you that even in the darkest moments, there's something positive to discover and grow from. They help you see the bright side when things feel really difficult.

Bee

Bees are everywhere in the world, and one kind of bee, the honeybee, is valuable to many spiritual beliefs. Bees help plants grow by spreading pollen, and humans get sustenance from fruits and vegetables because of them. Honeybees are also famous for their teamwork, how they work together for the greater good, and the unique patterns of their honeycombs. They make sweet-smelling beeswax, which people use to make candles. They also make honey from flower nectar. Bees show you how life can be sweet and rewarding when you work together and put in effort. Did you know there are thousands of bee types all over the world? Some don't make honey, but they're still important pollinators in their own homes. This reminds you to create new things or spread ideas, just like bees help plants grow.

Beetle

Dung beetles are the only bugs that use the Milky Way to find their way.
https://unsplash.com/photos/a-green-bug-sitting-on-top-of-a-white-flower-mMnckv9Dn6k

Beetles have been revered in different cultures, particularly the dung beetle. It has a special name, Scarabaeus sacer, which is Latin in origin, "sacer" means "sacred" or "revered." In ancient Egypt, the dung beetle, or scarab, was seen as a symbol for Khepri, the god of the dawn. Just as the dung beetle pushes a ball of dung, Khepri pushes the sun up each day, bringing light and warmth to the world. This also makes the scarab a symbol of new beginnings, creativity, change, and moving from dark to light. It's also connected to the fire element, which stands for passion and creativity. The scarab was so popular that people made jewelry and other things shaped like scarabs in ancient Egypt.

It might sound strange to respect a bug that eats waste, but dung beetles are actually really interesting. They can roll a ball of dung ten times heavier than them, and they're the only bugs that use the Milky Way to find their way. If you've ever seen a dung beetle roll its ball over a place full of sticks and leaves, you know how strong and determined they are.

Butterfly

Butterflies are living works of art.
https://unsplash.com/photos/IC8zpKz6qF0

Butterflies are living works of art. They've been part of gardens, art, and even jewelry for a really long time. These delicate creatures bring a feeling of lightness, inspiration, and happiness. They remind you that everything can change and become something beautiful. Butterflies show both strength and fragility. They have very delicate wings and only drink flower nectar, yet some, like the monarch butterfly, travel thousands of miles even though they seem too fragile to do so.

People in different cultures think of butterflies as connected to the soul. They start out as caterpillars and then transform completely into butterflies. It's a magical journey. Some think butterflies represent the soul that's inside you during life and even after death. Others see them as free spirits of those who have passed away. Either way, butterflies teach you about change, growth, and becoming something new inside.

Change doesn't always come easy. Even if it's necessary or feels good later, going through change can be tough. It takes bravery and belief to let go of the old and create something new. You can feel sad about what's changing and ask for help as you go through it. In these times, butterflies remind you that you can transform and grow like they do.

Cat

Cats are known for being dignified and graceful.
https://unsplash.com/photos/Tn8DLxwuDMA

House cats are the only cats that live closely with people as pets. They're loved for their companionship and cuteness. They might sleep a lot, but when they hear a noise or see something moving, they turn into hunters, like leopards or jaguars. They're good at caring for themselves outside and can find food by catching small animals. Cats are known for being dignified and graceful. People say they always land on their feet, and while that's not totally true, they can often twist their bodies in the air and land safely. This makes you think about being able to handle tough situations in your life.

Cats are curious animals, which is where the saying "curiosity killed the cat" comes from. Sometimes, their curiosity gets them into trouble, but it also helps them discover new things. They remind you to be curious and explore but also to be careful. Cats have a special mystery about them. The way they move and watch things around them is fascinating. In ancient stories, like those from Egypt, cats are even considered magical.

Chameleon

A chameleon wears its magic on the outside for all to see.
https://unsplash.com/photos/g_Kde88IlvE

A chameleon wears its magic on the outside for all to see. It changes colors, blends in, and hides in the most mystical way. Chameleons have long tongues that they shoot out to catch food and can even grab onto tree branches with their tails. Their eyes can look at two things at once, which helps them look out for predators. All these talents make the chameleon one of nature's most amazing and unusual animals. The chameleon is like a middleman in the animal world. It always looks for food and tries not to become someone else's dinner. Their life is about survival, but the chameleon teaches you that you can meet your needs differently. Sometimes, taking care of yourself feels boring or tiring. Just like the chameleon changes its colors, you can change how you do things and make it exciting. This means that you need to be open to new ideas, embrace your unique self, and be willing to see things differently. You might feel stuck in your routine, but the good news is you can get unstuck pretty easily.

Chicken

Chickens used to be rare in cities, but now they're becoming popular again.
https://unsplash.com/photos/auijD19Bvq8

When you think of a chicken, you think of the loud crowing of roosters, which you often hear in movies and shows as a signal for the start of a new day. Roosters make their noise at different times, but it's become a famous sign of morning, a time to wake up, get going, and begin the day with a fresh perspective. Even though it's not exactly scientific, there's a special meaning behind it that relates to your journey.

Chickens used to be rare in cities, but now they're becoming popular again. People keep them in their backyards for fresh eggs, which can be considered a symbol of new beginnings, just like the rooster's crow in the morning. Throughout history, eggs have stood for possibilities, starting anew, and creation. Many stories talk about a big bird or a special egg that gave birth to the universe or the world. Eggs are important in celebrations of spring, a time when things grow and become new again. Baby chicks also remind you of how delicate and happy new life can be.

Cow

Cows stay close to the ground, moving slowly and calmly, and this shows you how to be present and steady.
https://unsplash.com/photos/RxHhxWnXmNs

For thousands of years, cows have been beside humans, holding a special place in the holy writings of many religions. Hindus, for example, think cows are sacred, and in some parts of India, they can't be killed. In ancient Egypt, cows were connected to making things grow. They even linked cow-like qualities to goddesses like Hathor, who was all about joy, love, and beauty. Sometimes, people don't really appreciate cows and might see them as silly or funny. However, you should remember how important and calm they are, especially when they're taken care of with kindness and care. Cows stay close to the ground, moving slowly and calmly, and this shows you how to be present and steady. Cows have an interesting way of eating, too. They do something called "cud chewing," where they save food in their stomach and then regurgitate it to chew it properly. It's a good lesson for today's fast-paced life. Sometimes, you should put things aside and return to them later to learn and understand better.

Crow

Crows are smart and curious, known for solving problems and being a bit mischievous.

Crows are smart and curious, known for solving problems and being a bit mischievous. They represent wisdom, memory, and the mysteries of life. Even though they might sometimes be linked to dark things like death or war, they also bring magical energy and healing. In the medicine wheel, birds are connected to the mind, and crows are part of a smart group called Corvidae. These birds are so smart that they can even use tools, like sticks, to play with or to get food.

In Norse stories, the god Odin had two raven friends who whispered important secrets in his ear. In some Native American tales, the raven is a clever creator who fixed the sun, moon, and stars and even brought fire to people. Crows work together to solve problems and find food. They're quick and lively and might even bring little gifts to people they like. By watching them, you can learn that using your creative thinking can help you do things you never thought possible.

Deer

Deer are truly magical creatures.
https://unsplash.com/photos/INjjhMuzo6M

Deer are truly magical creatures. Their graceful movements have inspired people for a very long time. A powerful stag with big antlers has been a symbol of strength and honor. When deer move, they have this graceful fluidity that makes them seem to dance with beauty, whether in the woods or open fields.

To connect with a deer, you must match your energy to theirs. This special moment is precious because it could easily be disturbed – deer are easily startled. You become like them, silently aware of your body and everything around you. It's a lot like mindfulness. Deer don't make a noise. They just look at you, their ears moving to catch every sound. Then, they might suddenly run away, quickly and lightly.

Dove

The dove has stood for beauty, peace, grace, and communication for centuries.
https://unsplash.com/photos/6XcziMmkNgQ

For centuries, the dove has stood for beauty, peace, grace, and communication. In places like Mesopotamia and Greece, doves were linked with goddesses of love and beauty like Inanna-Ishtar and Aphrodite. They bring peace and good news. In the Bible, Noah sent out a dove to see if the flood was over, and it came back with an olive branch, a sign of peace. Hebrew and Christian stories also connect the dove to the spirit of God or the Holy Spirit. You can find it in all kinds of art, from religious to everyday creations.

The dove belongs to the air part of the medicine wheel in the north. It's a *teacher of teachers*. Many important human teachers share dove-like qualities: they see clearly and spread messages of peace and divine love far and wide. You don't need to be a peace master to connect with dove wisdom. Just remember that doves are messengers, usually bringing good news. Keeping communication open can help settle arguments and bring peace. It can also help you get closer to nature.

Eagle

The eagle symbolizes immense strength.
https://unsplash.com/photos/NEvS5lHyrlk

In both nature and human stories, the eagle symbolizes immense strength. With their big beaks, strong talons, and mighty wings, eagles command attention and have a serious look that takes in everything around them. Throughout history, eagles have been linked to nobility and even shown as symbols of military strength and pride. When you need to tap into your inner strength and stand firm in your beliefs, the eagle is a great friend to have by your side.

Eagles rule the skies and are top contenders in the world of the mind. Your mind is the key to shaping your own life story and contributing to the bigger picture of the world. Sometimes, you might forget how powerful your mind can be and think things outside your environment control you. However, the eagle reminds you that's not true. Your mind is a tool that keeps working, creating stories whether you know it or not. When you learn to use this tool in your best interest and express what you really mean, your mind becomes as strong as the eagle.

Elephant

Elephants build strong friendships and look after each other in their family groups.
https://unsplash.com/photos/QJbyG6O0ick

The elephant has fascinated and earned the respect of humans for ages, and they are seen as kind, strong guardians. They move calmly through the world, showing you the values of dignity, seriousness, and inner power. It's interesting—despite their big size and thick skin, elephants are really sensitive to touch, pressure, and even vibrations. Through their feet, they can "hear" the vibrations of other elephants and things happening miles away. Their trunks are like a treasure trove of smell and touch. In some religions in Asia, elephants are considered gods. For instance, there's Ganesha in India. Ganesha has a human body and an elephant head, representing wisdom, removing obstacles, and fresh beginnings.

Elephants build strong friendships and look after each other in their family groups. Like humans, dolphins, and chimps, elephants help their sick friends and family and feel sad when someone they love dies. While they can be aggressive under certain situations or when protecting their young, they're often playful and curious. The leader of an elephant group is usually a wise elder, often a grandmother. They teach you the value of friendship, strength not in size but kindness, and protecting one's own.

Fox

Foxes are clever, adaptable, sneaky, and quick.
https://unsplash.com/photos/xUUZcpQlqpM

Foxes are clever, adaptable, sneaky, and quick. They have a wild, mysterious air about them. While not as big and fearsome as bears or wolves, they're just as smart and capable. Foxes often get portrayed as tricky, sneaky, and sly, perhaps due to their sharp, alert faces or how they sometimes bother or hunt small animals. Their ability to move silently adds to their cunning reputation, making them like classic tricksters.

Like the fox, tricksters have deep wisdom, but it's not always straightforward. They teach in a kind of hidden, sideways manner, and things might not always be what they appear. In stories, foxes and other tricksters like coyotes and crows are known for tricking important figures out of valuable things, only to give those things to regular people later. They don't always come out on top, though. Tricksters can also make themselves look foolish and embarrassed, but they find a way to shake it off and keep going.

Goat

The goat shows you a different kind of fearlessness that doesn't require you to charge into battle or conquer enemies.

Goats are fearless creatures, but their fearlessness isn't about being aggressive like mighty predators like wolves or lions. Instead, goats fearlessly navigate their world with agility, sure-footedness, curiosity, and a strong determination to break free from boundaries if they can find a way to climb out.

In this modern society, people often carry heavy loads of paralyzing fears. You're hyper-aware of dangers lurking everywhere, which makes you hesitant to take risks or try new things. This can keep you confined and prevent you from exploring new horizons. The goat shows you a different kind of fearlessness that doesn't require you to charge into battle or conquer enemies. Instead, it's about having the courage and confidence to take small steps, one at a time. By doing so, you gradually ascend higher and higher, just like climbing a mountain.

Horse

Horses are renowned for their speed and endurance.
https://unsplash.com/photos/0F9oVQ3x2ak

Horses have been an integral part of human life and culture for thousands of years, with evidence of the partnership dating back to ancient times. While most horses are now domesticated, a few wild ones still roam. They have long played crucial roles in transportation, farming, hunting, and construction while being linked to gambling and war. In many ways, horses have contributed to shaping human civilization.

Not only are they practical allies, but they also hold a special place in mythology. They are the inspiration for mythical creatures like Pegasus, the hippogriff, and the unicorn. In Tibetan spirituality, the wind horse symbolizes the human soul and represents good fortune.

Horses are renowned for their speed and endurance. They can be both fierce fighters and brave companions. Riding a horse provides a unique sense of freedom and empowerment, even being used therapeutically. Horses have a remarkable ability to connect deeply, seemingly understanding human emotions and responding to inner selves. The bond between a horse and a person can be profound, offering a sense of purpose and completeness on life's journey.

Jaguar

Jaguar energy demands respect and requires skill to harness.
https://unsplash.com/photos/RgKsNlZJH8s

The jaguar, the largest native cat in America, holds significance in various Native American cultures like the Maya, Aztecs, and Toltecs. In Aztec civilization, jaguar warriors were an esteemed class who believed they gained the jaguar's strength in battle. The jaguar was sacred to the Aztec god Tezcatlipoca, associated with night, beauty, and war.

Wars and conflicts often arise from deeper fears and unexamined collective beliefs. A spiritual aspect of war involves battling your own internal conflicts and societal conditioning. Some, like Toltec warriors, engage in an ongoing battle to reveal their true selves, uphold their word, and stay connected to their inner life force.

Large predators like jaguars symbolize this battle. Their cunning and determination offer valuable lessons. Jaguar energy demands respect and requires skill to harness. Skilled warriors focus intensely on the present moment, knowing distractions could have life-altering consequences. Just as jaguars embody strength and focus, you can draw on their essence to navigate your inner battles and life's challenges.

Lion

Lions symbolize power, leadership, and fierceness in many ancient and modern cultures.
https://unsplash.com/photos/HZflGaOEzkI

With their majestic gold and bronze manes and graceful strength, lions symbolize power, leadership, and fierceness in many ancient and modern cultures. They are linked to royalty and often associated with the sun because of their radiant eyes, golden coats, and dark male mane resembling the light and shadows of the sun's rays. In ancient Egypt, lioness goddesses like Sekhmet represented the sun's fierce energy.

Lions are skilled hunters, capable of sudden bursts of speed and coordinated group hunts under the cover of darkness. While they are impressive predators, their success rate is around 25 percent, and they sometimes claim prey killed by smaller hunters. Their energy-conserving naps contribute to their royal reputation, reminiscent of house cats.

The lion's regal demeanor, strength, and power have led to its role as a symbol of kingship and leadership globally. Lion sculptures guard temple entrances and accompany deities as protectors. A successful leader embodies the lion's qualities—majesty, courage, and the ability to balance strength with grace.

Owl

The owl serves as a reminder that by attuning yourself to the natural world and trusting your own intuition, you can expand your awareness of the present moment.

https://unsplash.com/photos/tpxnuebsv28

Since ancient Greece, the owl has been seen as a guardian of knowledge and a companion to Athena, the goddess of wisdom. In certain cultures, owls are viewed as ominous symbols of death or messengers of ill intent. Some tales portray them not as birds but as spectral beings making eerie hoots and screeches. However, as with all teachings, you have the power to interpret and discern what holds significance for you. Chances are, you've experienced moments in your life when you received a mysterious "feeling" or surge of insight about a person, a potentially risky situation, or an exciting opportunity. Within you resides a wisdom that may not always be consciously recognized. The owl serves as a reminder that by attuning yourself to the natural world and trusting your own intuition, you can expand your awareness of the present moment.

Peacock

Peacocks command attention with their unique and striking appearance.
https://unsplash.com/photos/_7S3tOs424o

Peacocks command attention with their unique and striking appearance. They proudly display themselves, moving with a sense of purpose, as if saying, "Look at me!" Their extravagant appearance and confident demeanor make them a symbol of extravagance, splendor, and grandeur. However, peacocks are about more than just appearance. They also possess a protective instinct. They fiercely defend their territory and have even been used as a defense against snakes like cobras and rattlesnakes, which may pose a threat to livestock and people.

With their distinctive shrieking calls, peacocks seem to announce that this is a time for celebration, joy, and lively expression. They encourage you to proudly showcase your accomplishments, find delight in colors and creativity, engage in dance and music, and spread happiness.

Shark

The fear of sharks stems from the elemental aspect of their energy.
https://unsplash.com/photos/SFq3STsAKgc

Shark energy is a symbol of unwavering focus, heightened sensory awareness, powerful fluid grace, and mastery of the water—an element closely tied to emotions on the medicine wheel. The fear of sharks stems from the elemental aspect of their energy. Your emotions can feel like an unseen and unpredictable depth, influenced by currents beyond your control. Just as spending all our time on the surface makes us vulnerable to emotional ambushes, neglecting buried or unprocessed emotions can disrupt our equilibrium and cause harm. However, diving beneath the surface to confront and understand your feelings gives you the strength to navigate your inner world with the same ease as a shark in deep waters.

Spider

Spiders are renowned for their skill in building intricate webs, symbolizing all life's interconnectedness.
https://unsplash.com/photos/UUdJ-0LQs0M

Spiders have multiple legs, fang-like structures, and the ability to move swiftly or drop from above. Spiders are renowned for their skill in building intricate webs, symbolizing all life's interconnectedness. In indigenous cultures of America, spiders are associated with creation and creativity. Approaching spiders with respect can provide you with valuable teachings. Visualize a spider's orb web in the morning, adorned with dew droplets that glisten in the sunlight. This image reflects life's intricate beauty and delicate balance, reminding you of the interconnectedness of all living beings and the importance of respecting and appreciating the natural world around you.

Wolf

Wolves are animals that people in many cultures have respected and even feared.

Wolves are animals that people in many cultures have respected and even feared. They're known for being strong, great hunters, and for sticking together as a family. When you think of a wolf, you might hear their howling in your mind and imagine them under a bright full moon. Even though wolves don't really howl at the moon, the moon is still important in their stories.

Wolves usually live and hunt in groups called packs. But you might have heard the phrase "lone wolf," which means a wolf on its own. Being a lone wolf is being independent and solo for a while. It can be a bit challenging and sometimes risky, but it can also be a time to learn and grow. Eventually, lone wolves often join new groups or start their own. So, lone wolf wisdom can teach you about finding your own path and being brave when doing things independently.

Chapter 4: Calling in Your Power Animal

Working with the spirit world can be dangerous. You would not just walk into the middle of a crime-ridden major city and wave around your expensive phone and $ 10,000 in cash. There is much that can be explored in that major city, but you will take the necessary precautions to ensure you are safe. The modern spiritual movement has caused some of the deepest traditions to be commodified, repackaged, and misunderstood. Anyone with a YouTube channel and some feathers in their hair can now claim the title of Shaman or spiritual healer.

Therefore, it is essential to tread carefully and do extensive research before attempting to call on your power animals. You are in a submissive position when approaching your power animal. The animal is your teacher, and you are the student. Think of meeting your power animal as seeing a great aunt whom you have not spoken to in over a decade. She is still your family, but the relationship might be a little estranged. Her age puts her in a position of power because she is an elder. You wouldn't approach her recklessly or playfully like you would a peer or a friend. A certain level of respect would need to be maintained throughout the interaction.

Spirits are not human. They do not work according to the same social norms as people. When communing with the spiritual reality, the protocol must conform to a strict set of rules and principles. If you were to meet members of the royal family in the UK, you would get briefed on what you can or cannot do. They may even go as far as to tell you what you can wear or say. Similarly, meeting power animals comes with regulations you must abide by for your safety and to foster a good relationship with the spirit.

The unseen realm is complex. Western media and its influence have resulted in many viewing the spiritual world as angels versus demons. The spiritual realm has a variety of entities, beings, materials, and lifeforms. Some are evil, some are good, some are a bit of both, and others are neither. Good spirits can harm you. If you were running full speed in a crowded room, you may trip over someone's legs. That person hurt you, but it was not their fault. Your actions resulted in your pain. When you move inappropriately in the spirit world, you can be hurt in similar ways.

Introducing Yourself to Your Power Animal

Ancient Shamanic traditions work with energy exchanges, reverence, and honor. You and your power animal have known each other over many lifetimes, so this is more of a reintroduction. You will receive signs of your powerful animal in your waking and sleeping life. You may be dreaming about a raven, to wake up and find one sitting on your window sill. Your power animal will give you repeated signs to ensure you get the message. It is less you are calling your power animal than it is your power animal calling you because you are now ready.

Dreams of power animals calling you have similar themes. The animal will beckon you to follow it or tug at one of your body parts. You will be able to tell that it is your power animal because no matter how frustrated it grows in the dream due to your reluctance to follow it, the animal will not harm you. Power animals also tend to appear in surreal worlds. Sometimes, your dreams are very similar to the waking world, and other times, they are completely unrelated to any laws of physics people understand. Power animals will meet you in spaces that are otherworldly in your dream. For example, you may see a bear in a large, empty void.

Power animals are closely tied to your life purpose. You may encounter multiple power animals over your lifetime as you transition into different phases. Power animals make their appearance to usher you into a new reality. Different animals specialize in different areas of life. If you are a police officer or work in law enforcement, you may encounter a power animal dealing with strength. If you are creative, you may encounter a power animal focused on intuition.

The two main things to remember when meeting your power animal are to show respect and to be open to receiving guidance. Arrogance can turn a power animal against you and bring all kinds of turmoil into your life. Power animals are not wicked for allowing upheaval but are like a parent disciplining their child as a wake-up call.

Setting Intentions

Ritual is all about intention. Going into spiritual practice blindly without setting any intentions can send you on a chaotic rollercoaster ride. A lot can be learned in this chaos, but a lot more can also go wrong. Therefore, setting your intention when meeting your power animal is essential. The intention in the case of a power animal would be the question or questions that you would like to ask the spirit. It is better to go with one question instead of multiple questions because it allows the message to come through clearly.

Your intentions will be reflected in your offerings and the tools you decide to use. For example, if you are contacting your power animal, asking for transformation, you might use new moon water. Place a glass jar filled with water under the new moon to make new moon water. This water can then be sprayed or sprinkled onto your body as you recite your intention in any sphere of life. If you are consulting your power animal for financial abundance, you might incorporate some coins into your ritual. You can bury the coins and recite your intentions.

For a beginner just getting used to working in the spiritual realm, a great way to set intentions is by writing them down. Sometimes, it can be hard to remember your intention when you are in the middle of a ceremony, so writing it down will help you to internalize it better. Writing is also a way to think more deeply, so by inscribing your intention, you put more mental and physical energy into the process. The intention you wrote can then be folded up and burnt to release it. You can include numbers in the process by folding the paper a certain number of times. For example, if you were born on the 4th of a month, you will fold the paper four times. It is your intention, so get creative with introducing it into the ceremony for meeting your power animal.

When setting your intention, especially in the beginning, remember that you want to establish a bond. If you just met somebody, you would not make requests straight away. Furthermore, your power animal is a guide, not a genie. You are meant to listen more than you ask. Your desires might not align with your life's purpose, so you might ask your power animal for advice that could lead you astray. When creating your intention, remember that you are approaching your spirit to learn.

Keep your intention simple. Creating a convoluted and overcomplicated intention will cause chaotic results. Spirits are not human, so they may not understand the nuances of human life. Power animals do not see the world the same way you do. Therefore, be specific with your intention. Limit it to one sentence or question so you can build focus around it as you enter the ritual space. The simpler your intention is, the easier it will be to find the guidance you need.

Creating a Sacred Space

Offerings are important for creating a sacred space.
https://unsplash.com/photos/GNmUqW5AgA8

It is best to meet your power animal in nature because the Shamanic traditions from which the concept of animal spirits stems are closely intertwined with the natural world. Sound and light are the foundations of the universe. Everything holds a vibration, and all humans see are light reflections bouncing off objects. So, sound and light must be a part of any sacred space. In the Shamanic traditions, sound and light show up in the forms of drumming, chanting, and making a fire. If you cannot set a full-on fire and bang loudly on drums because of social or geographical restrictions, try electronically-played Shamanic singing and light some candles.

Offerings are important for creating a sacred space. Shamanism is a system of exchange. You must contribute to get something out, even in spiritual matters. Shamanistic cultures grew out of communal exchange systems that starkly contrast with the current individualistic system. The spirits you engage are part of your community, so in the same way, they will help you; they also need your assistance. Your offerings must be valuable to you, or they can be what the power animal would enjoy. For example, if your power animal is a bear, you can offer fish and berries. You can offer silver or metallic trinkets if your power animal is a crow.

How you present yourself to your power animal in terms of your physical appearance is also important to create a sacred space. Some practitioners of Shamanistic traditions practice in the nude, but that is too much for many people. When you enter the sacred space, take off your shoes and wear clothes that symbolize the power animal you are connecting with. For example, if you are connecting with a reindeer, you will wear horns, but if you are contacting a jaguar, you will wear black faux fur. You can be extravagant with your attire or keep it simple. A t-shirt with the animal printed on it also shows an appropriate degree of reverence. You can use colors in your attire to connect as well. Pure black or pure white represents a blank slate, like a newborn. Shamanism is steeped in honor of nature and ancestors. So, including red as well is appropriate as it represents your bloodline.

The boundaries of your sacred space should be clear. You can establish them physically by drawing a circle with ash, soil, or salt, or you can imagine them in your mind. Another way to create the borders of your sacred space is by using natural elements like plants or setting up beautiful decorations using cloths and candles. When crafting the sacred space, you will invite your power animal in to make use of all your senses. Be mindful of the sounds you create, the sights you see, what you smell, and what you feel. Make-up and face paint are great ways to involve texture in your ceremony because of how it feels on your skin. You can use the paint to mimic the animal you are connecting to.

Cleansing

Cleansing is a core element of most ancient rituals. If you were going on a date, you would not show up unwashed, with bad breath, or wearing stained clothes. You would be as fresh and clean as possible to make a good first impression. You can use salt and water to cleanse yourself spiritually. Rinse your hair, your beard if you have one, your hands, elbows, feet, knees, and face. Then rinse out your mouth and the inside of your nose. You can apply some holy oil to the same body parts once you are done. Any vegetable oil can be used as long as you have blessed it with words of affirmation like "I ask that you cleanse me and guide me through the journey to meet and connect with my power animal." Then, you can use incense like palo santo or sage to cleanse you further. Make sure to wave the smudging stick all around your body to cleanse every part of it.

Meditation and Visualization

Meditation and visualization are the most important components of meeting your power animal because the animal spirit will meet you in a visionary space.
https://unsplash.com/photos/NTvBbu66_SI

Meditation and visualization are the most important components of meeting your power animal because the animal spirit will meet you in a visionary space. This visionary space is easily entered when you go into a trance. Trances can be induced with ecstatic singing, chanting, dancing, and drumming. It is best to enter these spaces being guided by a Shaman or traditional healer because they know the spirit world and are familiar with what you may encounter. Sometimes, having a Shaman guide to meet your power animal is impossible. You can take a solitary journey, but there could be some difficulties due to a lack of knowledge of the spiritual realm.

A traditional healer in Africa was going through his initiation, and part of it was staying in a grass hut for two weeks without any contact with other people. Every morning, the guiding healer would come and leave a gallon and a half of water in front of the hut opening, the only time the traditional healer got to briefly speak to someone. One night, a heavy storm hit, and the hut was flooded. The initiate had to sit in one corner of the hut to remain dry. That night, a giant spider entered the hut and sat in the opposite corner. The spider scared the initiate, making his stay a bit more difficult. However, once he accepted that the spider would not hurt him, the process became a lot easier. The spider brought him comfort. The following night, he dreamt about the spider, and it guided him to become a skilled traditional healer. Through the altered state of fasting and light suppression, the initiate could enter a visionary state to communicate with his spirit animal.

Going through an ordeal like this may be too extreme for an individual and is not recommended without the appropriate help and expertise. Therefore, breath control and meditation is the calmest and safest way to meet an animal guide. Once you have cleansed yourself and entered your sacred space, sit or lie comfortably and close your eyes. The following visualization and meditation will help you meet your power animal:

With your eyes closed, take a few deep breaths in and out. At this point, you can play some calming meditation music or Shamanic chanting. Allow your thoughts to run wild while you are breathing. Focus on your breath, and do not judge your thoughts. You will notice that your thoughts will start looping, and eventually, they will slow down and become at ease if you keep focusing on your breath.

While still breathing consciously and deliberately, in through your nose and out through your mouth, begin imagining that you are sitting in the penthouse of a tall tower. You exit the penthouse door to find long, winding steps into the darkness.

Keep breathing as you slowly walk down the long spiraling stairway. There is a door at the bottom of the stairs. You open the door to see a vast forest with a lot of greenery and a path going deep into the woods. Follow that path.

Focus on your breathing. You continue walking down the path. You see a giant lake. Swim across the lake until you get to the other side. Imagine how the icy water feels on your skin. Once you get to the other side of the lake, there is a giant mountain. As you keep breathing consciously, climb up the mountain. When you reach the mountain's peak, you will find a deep cave. Walk into the cave's darkness until you meet your power animal, who will be ready to commune with you. This exercise may take some time, and you might not meet your power animal on the first try. Be ready to practice, and be patient. You will meet the spirit when the time is right.

Chapter 5: Journeying to Find Your Power Animal

The Shamanic journey is an age-old spiritual practice open to everyone. It connects practitioners to the spiritual world, where they can receive guidance and healing. You can also take this journey to find and connect with your power animal. Wondering how to do it? While it takes some practice to master it, journeying is akin to dream work (interpretation of spiritual signs in dreams) and similar meditative practices. Have you ever had a dream so vivid you could've sworn you've truly been in that place/situation you've experienced in the dream-vision? You could remember everything from the smells to the color of the walls, and everything felt immensely familiar. Journeying is almost the same, except you're taken to this almost dreamlike state while still awake. The explanation behind this is simple. Everything in the universe is connected, and spiritual journeys celebrate this interconnectedness. If you view yourself as a part of this web, it's much easier to cross the divide between the realms in waking life. Shamans believe that there is a balance in nature. Besides letting you experience the togetherness of everything in nature, Shamanic journeying provides an understanding of your actions' impact on your surroundings and other living creatures. You can find your own balance or contribute to the overall balance in nature by connecting to your power animal and following its guidance. You can harness its power to heal and restore balance to other people's lives. In ancient times, the primary role of Shamanic journeying was finding tools for healing. Spiritual imbalances cause physical and mental illnesses. By reinstating the balance, Shamans restore the health of those suffering from ailments. By seeking guidance from your power animal, you can do the same.

The Shamanic Journey

Since the beginning of recorded history, the Shamanic journey has been initiated and accompanied by music, which helps the Shaman (and anyone else participating) enter an altered state of consciousness. Some practitioners use chanting, prayers, flutes, rattles, and herbal medicine (plants that enhance the altered state of consciousness) - although the latter is rarely advised or preferred by modern practitioners.

Rhythmic drumming is still frequently used to induce Shamanic journeys because it is repetitive and creates relaxation-inducing brain frequencies. Traditional Shamanic practices hold drums in high esteem, and every culture has its own drumming rhythm and instrument they use. This instrument is one of the Shaman's essential tools, so novices are often instructed to meditate to Shamanic drumming when preparing for their first spiritual journeys. Listening to the steady rhythm of drums makes it easier to embrace whatever you experience while in an altered state of consciousness.

The Three Shamanic Worlds

Shamans divide the spiritual realm into three parts: the Lower world, the Middle world, and the Upper world. Each of them can be visited and explored during a Shamanic journey. Experienced practitioners are often accompanied by a spiritual helper (like a power animal) on their journeys. However, if you're yet to find your power animal, you'll likely meet them in one of the Shamanic worlds. Shamans use the Axis Mundi (known as the World Tree in Shamanic traditions) to navigate the different worlds. As its name suggests, the Axis Mundi grows at the center of the three worlds. To visit them, you need to follow its trunk. You're in the middle of this trunk - in the Shamanic Middle World.

However, to see it in its entirety, you must look a little closer. Think of this task as one of those brain teasers where you must find the differences between two pictures. The Middle World looks similar to the mundane world but includes all spiritual aspects and dimensions. It encompasses the mundane realm, the worlds of nature's creatures, the spiritual elements of nature, and the future and the past facets of life on

Earth. Your power animal might drop you a couple of hints in this world, making it easier for you to pick them up.

Each of the three worlds vibrates in a singular atmosphere and offers different advantages to visitors. As you practice, you'll learn from experience which world is most suitable for your intentions. For example, if you want to request advice on a new project, you'll get the most valuable guidance from the Upper world. By contrast, if you want to heal spiritually, you'll journey to your power animal in the Lower world.

Many practitioners find that journeying to meet their power animal in the Lower world is valuable in supporting their mental or physical healing process. Moreover, the Upper world might reveal valuable lessons for reaffirming your intention to heal yourself or others. Given that the spiritual guides in this world operate in their own frequency, they might give you a fresh perspective on your situation. In this way, they help you find new ways to support yourself on your path. Through personal experience, the Shamanic journeyer will become more familiar with these worlds and their inhabitants. Through your journeys, you'll get to know the landscape and your power animal better and better.

Despite living closest to the Middle World, many practitioners find it the easiest to journey to the Lower World. In fact, this is where most beginners are instructed to travel when retrieving their power animal for the first time. To reach it, you'll descend deep into the lower part of the trunk of the Axis Mundi. This might sound complicated, but it doesn't have to be. You might have to visualize a long tunnel you enter through an opening in the earth, like a hole at the base of a tree, a staircase leading downward. In other words, you can view it as any natural opening that prompts your imagination to set you on the path toward the Lower World. One of the central aspects of this realm is its profound relationship with power and transformation. Hence, it's the best place to find your power animals. You'll find the most helpful, kind, compassionate, and loving creatures in this realm.

The Upper World is above the earthly realm. You can reach this world in the Shamanic trance journey by traveling higher and higher on the World Tree's trunk until you go beyond the stars. This realm has a much higher vibration than the Lower and Middle Worlds. The creatures of the Upper world are also often different in their vision and attributes. For example, a power animal you meet in the Upper World could offer more empowerment to distance yourself from challenging situations, allowing you to heal. This realm also reveals fantastic tools for gaining self-awareness and confidence. You can truly step up your healing game by discovering new, finer, and often more empowered parts of your being.

Meeting and Communing with One's Power Animal

Journeying with Shamans to Meet Your Power Animal

Power animals lurk in the spiritual world, and journeying there is a fantastic way to meet them. Shamans are highly knowledgeable of the spiritual world and well-versed in journeying. So, if you want to meet your power animal, ask a Shaman to accompany you on your quest. A Shaman will show you how to journey to the Lower World and help you identify your power animal based on their gifts. They'll also help you connect with them by asking the creature to either send a message to you or show themselves in any form. If you've already seen your power animal, working with a Shaman can help you establish communication with the animal so you can learn why they're in your life. While you can ask the shamans to journey themselves, the animals won't share their messages with them. They want to connect with and guide you as you navigate through life. They'll only appear to you because they'll know you're honoring your eternal bond with them.

Meditation for Deepening Your Consciousness

Meditation is another powerful way to calm your mind and open it up for receiving messages from your power animal. Meditation is a mindfulness technique focusing on deepening your breathing, which allows your mind to reach a deeper state of consciousness. It also ensures you won't run into any hindrances as you establish communication with your power animal.

Instructions:

1. Have a paper and a pen with you. Find a comfortable position and start breathing deeply until you feel relaxed. Once your body and mind are serene, you won't have any problems sensing your power animal's approach and reaching out to connect to them.

Find a comfortable position and start breathing deeply until you feel relaxed.

2. When you feel that your mind is free of prejudice, state your intention of gaining spiritual empowerment to meet your power animal. Having something to focus on will facilitate reaching the altered state of consciousness you're looking for. (If you lack experience with meditation, ask an experienced guide to lead you on this path.)

3. State your intention three more times. Have you noticed any signs pop up around you? If yes, note them down immediately.

4. When you are finished, read your notes and see if you pick up any patterns. Ask your gut how you feel about your experience. It will give you a clue on which signs to follow every time you practice this meditation.

The following real-life example highlights the power of meditation in finding one's power animal:

I found my power animal through a deep meditation session. I wasn't sure what to ask for when I decided to start meditating to find this guide, I just knew that meditation felt right for seeking a spiritual connection with them. So before my first session, I will just meditate with the intention of finding a power animal I can relate to. I knew that my power animal and I had much in common, so meditating on how I am like my power animal was the natural choice. I have a strong bond with my family and I am always there for them when they need me, so I focused on finding an animal with similar protective instincts and closeness to its pack or flock. During my first session, a white figure appeared in front of my (closed) eyes for a couple of seconds but soon disappeared. In the next session, the picture became clearer, and I knew it was a large white animal. Before my next session, I asked for a sign that the white animal was my power animal. Delving into my inner world, I focused strongly on my attention, and soon enough, there it was, a magnificent white wolf with the bluest eyes in the world in front of me. It sniffed the air by lifting its head toward me as if to greet me, and I had my answer; I'd met my power animal and established a connection with them. - Veronica

Visualization for Manifesting Power Animal Signs

Do you have something urgent to ask your power animal? Perhaps you have to make a potentially life-changing decision and want your animal's guidance. If yes, ask the creature to show a sign that'll help you decide. As you do, visualize your intention of receiving their message. It indicates to your power animal that you need their help urgently and prompts them to launch into action.

Instructions:

1. Prepare a soothing setting, perhaps with meditation music or drums.

2. As soon as you feel yourself relax, deepen and slow your breathing, and visualize yourself in a majestic natural scene. For example, you might imagine walking out of a forest into a sunlight clearing full of colorful wildflowers.

Visualize yourself in a majestic natural scene.

3. Pay close attention to every detail of the scenery before you. Can you feel the fresh scent of the pine trees? How about the feel of the sun's warmth on your skin?

4. Try to find a path leading into the depths of this world. If you find an entrance, take that path and see if a power animal appears. If it doesn't, ask them to send you signs.

5. As you leave the depths of the world, you might notice an animal that wasn't there before. Has a creature appeared to you several times in a row? If yes, they're likely your power animal. Or you might not see any animal at all. Ask them for a sign again and wait a little.

6. If the signs don't come right away, don't sit around until they do. Feel free to go about your day as usual, and let the animal come to you with the guidance you need. They will send those signs sooner or later.

Be on the Lookout for Their Signs

Power animals are unique, just like people are. They like different things and communicate differently as well. For example, some might send you messages or symbols through visions. Whereas others will reach out to you directly while you're meditating. Either way, if the message comes from your power animal, it will be hard to miss. After all, you have a unique bond with your power animal, which ensures you can decipher their signs. Sometimes, the messages will appear in the most unusual form because the animal knows this is the right way to reach you. This might be a dream that seemingly has nothing with it, yet it appears so frequently that it makes you wonder whether it's from the animal. Or, you might be thinking about an idea you would like confirmation of, and you hear a song on the radio that seems to answer your unspoken question. Look out for these random yet natural signs around you, and you'll soon start to notice them more and more.

Instructions:

1. Create a soothing environment with incense, candles, and meditation music/drumming.
2. Prepare to enter a (slightly) altered state of consciousness by breathing deeply and relaxing your mind and body.
3. Let yourself relax fully.
4. Visualize yourself in a natural environment, like a park.
5. Call on your power animal. If you see a creature, ask if they're your power animal and whether they have a message for you.

Here is a testimony that proves that looking out for signs from your power animal is a great way to facilitate your encounter with them:

I started reading about power animals as part of a spiritual journey I took after a painful divorce. I read about the power animals' ability to guide their charge through sad times, and I suddenly had a wish to meet my power animal. I never encountered it, but throughout the years, I always felt I had a powerful spiritual guide. So, after unsuccessfully trying to overcome the profound pain after my divorce, I started to ask for a sign from a power animal. I didn't ask them to show themselves. I only asked them to send me a sign that I would be okay and the pain would pass. I also began to pay more attention to my surroundings, trying to pick up signs that could come from my power animal. For three weeks, I was unsuccessful until I finally got my wish. One day, as I stepped out to my porch, I noticed a beautiful blue bird pecking at the railing. I had never seen this bird near my home before this, so it immediately caught my attention. When the same thing happened the next day, I started to suspect that this blue bird could be my power animal. Later the same day, I sent a silent request to my power animal, asking for a sign that I would heal. The next day, the bird was there again, but as I stepped out,

I flew closer to me, looked at me, and then flew away. The day, instead of the soulcrashing pain I usually felt waking up after the divorce, I felt hope. I knew then that the little bird was my power animal, and it told me that I would be all right. While the bird didn't come back the next day, from time to time, when I feel I need guidance or advice on my spiritual journey, all I need to do is ask, and the little blue bird appears on my porch. -Marianne

Asking Other Animals

Suppose a creature comes to you during meditation or in a vision multiple times, but you feel no indication that it's your power animal. In that case, they're likely showing you the path toward your true power animal. Have you heard someone saying they have several power animals? If you haven't yet, you probably will because many people encounter more than one animal throughout their lives. These creatures steered them toward the right path, so they mistakenly thought they were all power animals. When, in fact, all but one were helper animals that guide people toward their true power animal. Your power animal might also possess the gift of speaking through other creatures. If an animal appears to you during meditation only once, ask whether they are your guide. If they aren't, they'll help you reach the animal that is.

As the following testimony illustrates, following other animals on your journey can play its dividends:

> *"I was taking my second journey to meet my power animal - as the first one was unsuccessful. As I relaxed and reached the state where I could visualize the entrance to the spirit world, I decided to focus only on my intention and not let anything deter me this time. When I entered the Lower World, I met an animal to whom I felt no connection. I also met them last time, but I was too afraid to follow them without a connection or knowledge of where they might lead me. This time, however, I let them lead me. They took me to new places in the Lower World. As they did, I heard them whispering messages, counseling me on what to do when I met my power animal. Then, my true animal was revealed to me, and I was able to rely on their guidance further and further along the path of teaching and spiritual growth."* - Gabriel

Learn to Embrace Their Gifts

Some people are aware of their power animal being by their side from an early age. Others learn about the existence of these magnificent creatures later in life and decide to meet their own. Whichever your case is, when you decide to reach out to your power animal, be prepared to embrace their gifts in whatever form they come. It might not come in the way you would wish it to come, but your power animal's support will be what you need. Their unique power makes your power animals' gifts immensely valuable. They know what type of help you need, even if you don't. They also know how much push you require to make the changes on your own. You might think you need more or don't even know you need their help. However, they do and will readily grant it to you. Encountering your power animal can be a confusing experience. Still, always take their gifts as they come because they come that way for a reason - to foster an empowering bond with a friend you can hit up for advice for the rest of your life.

Here is a mediation to prepare yourself to accept your gifts when reaching out to the.

Instructions:

1. Begin the meditation by relaxing yourself. Breathe deeply for several minutes. Let the air in through your nose and release it through your mouth. Take longer with the exhale - this is key to total relaxation.

2. Announce your intention to meet with your power animal and receive their gifts. Say slowly and deliberately recite the following:

   "I am ready to welcome you into my life and have your blessings bestowed upon me."

3. If you know your power animal's name, say it. If not, simply invite them to come to you. Say:

   "I know your power. I'm opening myself to your strength and power."

4. If you have a specific gift in mind, describe it. The more precise you're in what you need, the easier you'll find your power animal, decipher its messages, and receive its gifts.

5. Feel yourself becoming one with the gift you're about to receive. Feel how your power animal is enveloping you with its light and love.

6. Give thanks to your helper by saying:

"Thank you for sharing your ancient wisdom with me, my friend."

Chapter 6: Power Animals and Dreams

The dream realm has always been filled with mystery.
https://unsplash.com/photos/v9X4-ACaPUs

Humans, animals, and even birds dream every time they go to sleep. All people dream, even if they don't remember them. The dream realm has always been filled with mystery. For centuries, dreams and sleep have always baffled scientists. They have been trying to uncover the secrets behind them, but they still can't find concrete answers.

One thing is certain: anything is possible in the dream realm. You can be a superhero, fight zombies, or be a famous rockstar. You won't think, "How did I get here?" Logic doesn't really factor in here, and anything is possible and believable. This makes dreams the perfect setting for your power animal to communicate with you. They can reveal themselves to you, send you messages, or offer guidance.

In the Shamanistic notion, power animals represent who you really are. When animals emerge from within a dream, the dreamer is initiated and is meant to accept the attributes and spiritual power of the animal. In other words, whatever qualities your power animal shows in your dreams, they reflect who you truly are. Pay attention to your dreams and notice all the details because there is a meaning behind everything you see.

This chapter covers the most common animal symbols in dreams, their interpretations, and methods to interpret animal dreams.

How Dreams Work

Have you ever wondered why you dream? You close your eyes, drift off to sleep, and suddenly, you are in the dream realm, running from a monster or living the life of your dreams with your soulmate. So, how do you dream?

Dreams are emotions, thoughts, or images people experience while sleeping. However, not all people dream the same way. For instance, some dream in black and white, while blind people dream about scents or sounds. However, most dreams are irrational and involuntary and evoke powerful emotions.

People dream during the REM (rapid eye movement) cycle, which takes place ninety minutes after you fall asleep. During this time, certain parts of your brain become active, allowing you to see, hear, move, and talk in your dreams. However, in reality, your body is sleeping, and your eyes are closed. Your brain is just processing sensory inputs to create the experience of dreaming.

Dreams stem from your subconscious mind. Everything you see, believe, feel, and experience in your waking life is stored in your subconscious, even things you aren't aware of or have forgotten about.

The subconscious is always awake, even when you aren't. However, it doesn't work like your conscious mind. It often thinks in metaphors and symbols. This is why dreams are often strange and unclear and require interpretation.

Shamans are very interested in dreams and believe they are a source of knowledge and magic. In shamanism, power animals call on Shamans in dreams to fulfill their purpose as healers or to rise as spiritual power leaders. The spirits can also give them healing powers or outward visions.

Shamans believe that in dreams, everything is alive and connected. Animal dreams are sacred and intuitive, usually speaking and offering wisdom. When you see a wolf or a lion in your dream, you aren't just seeing a wild animal. This is a spiritual dream because all animals are a force for good and play a significant role in the universe.

Shamans understand that animals appear in dreams not as themselves but as spirit guides or power animals. They can protect you, share their wisdom, or send you messages from the spirit realm. Shamans believe that all animal dreams have symbolic or personal meanings behind them. Understanding what they mean requires you to interpret them and understand their symbolic meanings.

Most Common Animal Archetypes in Dreams

This part covers animal archetypes that appear in dreams and their characteristics and symbolic interpretation. This information will give you an idea of which aspects of your personality your power animal represents.

Apes

Apes represent your primal instinct or the desire to cause trouble just to get attention.
https://unsplash.com/photos/tHEr4iqoWBQ

Apes represent your primal instinct or the desire to cause trouble just to get attention. They also symbolize relationships, friendships, and knowledge. Dreaming of an ape can mean you are struggling to deal with your overwhelming emotions.

Bats

Bats represent unpredictability, intuition, protection, power, and change. They also symbolize negatives like repressed emotions, insecurities, or fears you don't want to accept or face. Dreaming of a bat is a sign that you should embrace all sides of your personality: the good, the bad, and the ugly.

Media and literature have always linked bats with vampires and witchcraft because they are mysterious and dark. It is natural to be worried or afraid when you see one in your dreams.

However, bats are also associated with spirituality and can also symbolize change and growth. If your power animal is a bat, it will often come to you from the spiritual world to protect and guide you.

Bears

Bears represent protection, security, and strength.
https://unsplash.com/photos/BvSOxut6w6o

Bears represent protection, security, and strength. Seeing one in your dreams indicates you are either feeling defensive or safe. Dreaming of a bear indicates something is going on in your life, making you feel extra protective or highly sensitive. Perhaps someone has hurt your feelings, leading you to put up shields.

Butterflies

Butterflies symbolize rebirth, change, transformation, freedom, independence, joy, elegance, and peace. Dreaming of one is a sign that your life is about to change.

Cats

Since power animals are wild, you won't see a pet cat in your dreams but a wild one with much wisdom to give. Cats represent independence, a gentle nature, and curiosity, for which they are famous. If you have a cat, you will understand. They can also symbolize your instinctual nature of refusing to be tied down or domesticated. The dream tells you to follow your instincts or heart and not overthink every decision. It is a sign to try new things and take risks. Famous psychoanalyst Sigmund Freud said that dreaming of cats means you are experiencing tension in your waking life. It is trying to tell you to let go and free yourself.

Dogs

Dogs symbolize friendship, loyalty, and a loving personality.
https://unsplash.com/photos/2_3c4dIFYFU

Who doesn't love dogs? They are everyone's favorite pets. They symbolize friendship, loyalty, and a loving personality. However, your power animal will most likely appear as a wild dog, like a coyote or jackal. They stand as guards at the gateway of the subconscious, so they know your deepest secrets. Seeing a wild dog in your dreams indicates you are afraid to face your true feelings and would rather have them hidden in the subconscious. You believe if you express how you truly feel to others, they will take advantage of you. Wild dogs can also signify that you are sacrificing so much for others and not giving yourself enough time or attention.

The dream can also be a message from your power animal to stop acting too passively because you are pushing your loved ones away. You can also see a wild dog in your dreams if you are experiencing transformation.

Dolphins

Dolphins symbolize friendship, intelligence, playfulness, and gentle nature.
https://unsplash.com/photos/K6kZKJOmZrk

Just like dogs, dolphins are extremely popular and everyone's best friend. They even share many qualities with them, like loyalty and loving personality. Dolphins symbolize friendship, intelligence, playfulness, and gentle nature. They also represent your love for the people in your life and how easily you connect with others on a deeper level.

Dreaming of dolphins means that you are a wise individual who can live a successful and happy life.

Elephants

Elephants represent wisdom, patience, intelligence, strength, success, endurance, honor, perseverance, enlightenment, and spiritual growth. Although they are large animals and can trample a person to death, on the inside, they are very emotional beings, but they never forget. Dreaming of an elephant represents your strong emotions that can overpower the negative thoughts that prevent you from achieving your goals.

Elephants also indicate you are hurting and can no longer hide your pain. These feelings are powerful and overwhelming. Even though you bottle them up and try to ignore them, they consume you and affect your life in different ways. Since elephants have a strong memory, the dream can be a sign that you are struggling with letting go of the past. You can't forgive or forget, and it's haunting and tormenting you.

This message tells you that you can never run away from your feelings, and bottling them up isn't the answer. They can be destructive. You should find a healthy way to release these emotions and deal with them.

Fox

Foxes symbolize freedom, cleverness, independence, beauty, cunning, confusion, and fear. They have always been associated with magic and are believed to bring good luck and prosperity. However, dreaming of a fox can have negative meanings as well. It can be a sign that you are being manipulated or facing obstacles.

Horses

Horses represent freedom, enthusiasm, power, and a desire to win and are often associated with the spirit. They also symbolize communication or a link between your emotions and thoughts. This stems from the belief that horses have psychic abilities and can tap into their riders' thoughts. They can also be a sign of empowerment or that your life is out of control.

Lions

A lion symbolizes courage, strength, leadership, confidence, power, fearlessness, and dignity. It is also associated with a lack of conformity and a desire to be free from the shackles of society. Lions are also fierce protectors, so they can reflect your parenting side and a desire to protect your children, family, and friends. Dreaming about the king of the jungle indicates a situation in your life that is out of your control, and you should take charge and make some changes. It can also represent your self-worth or enthusiasm about your life.

Monkeys

Monkeys symbolize intellect, joy, curiosity, playfulness, transformation, creativity, mischievous behavior, and lack of control.
https://unsplash.com/photos/aXqlZFeVFrU

Monkeys symbolize intellect, joy, curiosity, playfulness, transformation, creativity, mischievous behavior, and lack of control. Dreaming about a monkey shows you are full of agility, freedom, and vitality, but you keep this side of yourself hidden. A monkey reflects your desire to run away from an average, rigid life that doesn't challenge you. It can also warn that someone in your life wants to harm you.

Snakes

Snakes can symbolize the poisonous side of your personality that you reject and repress to protect the people in your life.
https://unsplash.com/photos/f1q4NlVRYSc

No one wants to dream of snakes as most people believe they are associated with bad qualities like betrayal, immorality, deceit, evil, and temptation. However, they have positive and negative interpretations. Snakes can symbolize the poisonous side of your personality that you reject and repress to protect the people in your life. Denying any aspect of yourself, even the ugliest parts, will only hurt you the most. Perhaps this is a sign that you must come to terms with your darkness rather than deny it. It is the only way you will heal.

The positive meaning behind snakes in dreams is that they represent change, transformation, overcoming hardships, and the ability to let go. Dreaming of a snake indicates that you will give birth (if you are a woman), have a happy life, get promoted, start a new business, or achieve your dreams.

Tigers

Tigers symbolize power, fierceness, control, authority, and agility.
https://unsplash.com/photos/66zrT0qJ7Mc

Tigers symbolize power, fierceness, control, authority, and agility. Dreaming of a tiger can mean you are in a powerful position but are taking advantage of your high status. This is a sign that you should self-reflect on how you treat others. It can also be a sign of your inner strength. You have so much going on inside of you, and you should harness your abilities to accomplish your goals. Dreaming about a tiger can also indicate you will face threats, dangers, or challenges.

Unicorns

Unicorns symbolize purity, innocence, and regeneration.

DALL·E artificial intelligence; prompted by Artisaurus, CC0, via Wikimedia Commons: https://commons.wikimedia.org/wiki/File:Portrait_of_a_Unicorn.png

How great would it be if your power animal was a mythical creature like a unicorn? Unicorns symbolize purity, innocence, and regeneration. They represent good fortune and virginity and often appear in dreams to guide you and encourage you to keep going until you become the best version of yourself. A unicorn symbolizes your desire to fall in love or your selfish nature.

Wolf

Wolves represent unconditional love, companionship, intelligence, freedom, determination, courage, protection, and strength. They can also symbolize a primal and untamed side of your personality. Dreaming of wolves indicates you are scared or have just lost a job or a loved one. If you are in a relationship, the wolf dream is a sign that you miss your independence. This doesn't mean you want to break up with your partner but just wish you had freedom.

It also means you are hiding a part of your personality. Like the werewolf, you can't be your truest self around others.

Although each animal has its own characteristics and symbolic interpretation, the meaning can change depending on the context and your personal association with the animal. What is the animal doing? Is it trying to attack you? Is it protecting you? The animal's actions and behavior are relevant to dream interpretation.

Pay attention to all other details as well, like the location, theme, other people, etc. Notice your feelings. Are you happy, excited, sad, angry, etc.? In other words, don't only focus on the animal but also on yourself and everything else taking place in the dream.

For instance, a butterfly is a positive symbol representing change. However, if it appears in a negative context, this indicates your resistance to change. There is a difference between dreaming of a butterfly flying on a warm sunny day and dreaming about it lying on the ground in a gloomy, deserted area. Your power animal can also appear to reflect aspects of your personality or with a message to guide you.

Considering your personal association with the animal is also necessary for dream interpretation. Do you love the animal? Does it bring you good memories? Or are you terrified of it? For instance, two people dream about bears: one loves them while the other is terrified. Here, the bear will have a positive meaning for the person who loves it and a negative meaning for the other.

Therefore, the symbols and metaphors you see in dreams are open to many interpretations depending on various factors.

Interpreting Animal Dreams

Now that you have learned about the meaning behind different animals in dreams, discover how to interpret them.

Keep a Dream Journal

Keep a dream journal and a pen next to your bed to write down your dreams every morning. Remember to record your thoughts as soon as you wake up before you forget them. Include every detail, such as what the animal looked like, what it was doing, its emotions, the setting, and other people in the dream. You should also reflect on your feelings, thoughts, and reactions during the dream. If you have an artistic side, draw any peculiar symbols you see. After you finish recording it, check the meaning behind the animal you saw.

A dream journal will give you insight into your subconscious so you can recognize common symbols and patterns. You will also keep track of the messages your power animal is communicating to you.

Emotions in Dreams

Your emotions are key to interpreting your animal dreams. For instance, normally, you would be terrified if you saw a tiger in real life. However, if in your dream, you feel safe and protected, it has a positive interpretation. On the other hand, you may feel angry or scared when you see a unicorn. This indicates that the dream has a negative translation. For this reason, you should record your dream right after you wake up to remember your exact emotions to interpret your dreams better.

Visualization

If you don't remember your dreams, you will miss any encounters with your power animal and the messages they try to communicate to you. However, visualization is an effective technique to recall your dreams. This is also helpful when there are specific details you might have missed, or you want to improve your memory so you won't forget your dreams.

Visualization will work better when you sit in a quiet room with no distractions and close your eyes.

- **Scene Rehearsal Technique:** Visualize you are back in your dream and rehearse the events. If any details were missing in the dream, add them to the visualization scenario.

- **Dream Playback Technique**: Visualize your dream from beginning to end as if you are watching a movie. Immerse yourself in the experience and see if you have missed anything. Pay attention to your emotions, events you encountered, and other people in the dream. Practice this exercise daily to improve your memory so you can easily remember your dreams every day.

- **Sensory Visualization Technique:** Imagine the dream using your five senses to relive the whole experience. Remember the scents, sounds, sights, physical sensations, and taste. Employing your senses will make it easier to recall your dreams.

Personal Meaning of Animal Encounter

Think about your life, experiences, and emotions and how they are associated with the animal in your dreams. Connect how you felt in the dream to your current situation. You should also pay attention to the encounter with the animal: is it positive or negative?

Trust your intuition and embrace the process of connecting with your power animal through the realm of dreams with dedication and an open heart. Dreams give you a unique opportunity to communicate with your animal guide and develop a close relationship with them. Every night before you go to sleep, believe that you will either dream about your power animal or receive a message from them. Even if it doesn't happen right away, never give up.

Dreams are deeply personal. Even though there are common symbols and meanings behind everything you see, you are the only one who can truly interpret them.

Two people can look at the same painting, each with a different reaction. One might feel sad, tears flowing down their face, while the other might feel at peace and smile. It all depends on the person, their thoughts, current situation, life experiences, and how the painting makes them feel. Perhaps it brought positive memories to one while reminding the other of a loss. The same applies to interpreting dreams. One animal can be associated with a happy memory, while another can remind you of an unpleasant experience.

Interpreting dreams isn't just looking for symbols and their meaning. It is about self-reflection and considering your feelings and personal associations with the animal. Listen to your heart because it will never lead you astray.

You don't need to wait for your spirit guide to come to you in your dreams. You can take the initiative and control them yourself. This involves interesting techniques you will learn about in the next chapter.

Chapter 7: Meeting Your Power Animal through Dreams

Dreams bridge the conscious and subconscious mind, making them a powerful conduit for encountering one's power animal.

If there is a person or thought you can't get out of your head in your waking life, you may see them in your dreams. So, does that mean if you keep thinking about your power animal, you will dream about it at night? Well, yes and no.

Seeing your power animal in your dreams is possible if you think about it hard enough. However, why would you leave it to chance? There are things that you can do to facilitate the process. However, you may not see your power animal itself but a symbol representing it, so you should refer to the animal symbolism in the previous chapter.

This chapter discusses different methods to guide you to meet your power animal in the land of dreams.

Relaxation Techniques

Relaxation techniques include deep breathing, progressive muscle relaxation, yoga, and meditation.

https://unsplash.com/photos/TdrUCJU6VFs

Relaxation techniques include deep breathing, progressive muscle relaxation, yoga, and meditation. They can reduce tension in your body, calm your mind, and make you feel relaxed.

Do you know that stress and anxiety can impact your dreams? When you are rested, you will sleep well at night and have pleasant dreams. On the other hand, stress leads to disturbed sleep and nightmares.

Practice any of these relaxation techniques before bed for a good night's sleep and sweet dreams.

Deep Breathing Exercise

Deep breathing exercises slow down your breathing, lower your heart rate, and let the brain relax and unwind, which impacts your body and makes it ready for sleep.

Instructions:

1. Lie down in a comfortable position, on your bed or the floor.
2. Breathe normally for a few seconds.
3. Let go of all your thoughts and everything bothering you, and only focus on your breathing.
4. Take a long, deep breath through pursed lips, then slowly breathe out, releasing all the air from your lungs.
5. Keep breathing in and out of your abdomen while imagining it is a balloon filling with air as you inhale and emptying as you exhale.
6. Repeat the previous steps for five to 10 minutes.
7. Practice this exercise every night before bed.

Progressive Muscle Relaxation Exercise

This technique brings tension to the muscle and then releases it so you can experience complete relaxation.

Instructions:

1. Find a quiet room away from distractions.
2. Wear loose clothes and take off your shoes.
3. Sit in a comfortable position or lie down. Lying down is ideal if you want to fall asleep immediately after the exercise.
4. Take five deep and slow breaths.
5. Begin the exercise by tensing your muscles.
6. Focus on the muscles you want to work on (the steps are the same for all muscles).
7. Inhale slowly and deeply, then squeeze the muscles gently but hard while holding your breath for five seconds or until you feel the tension in your muscles.
8. It is normal to experience shaking or discomfort.
9. Try to avoid causing tension to the surrounding muscles. However, practice will teach you to focus only on the target muscles.
10. Now, you will relax the tensed muscles.
11. Let go of the muscles you are squeezing while breathing out. You should feel your muscles relaxing.

12. Notice the difference between tense muscles and relaxation.

13. Feel the relaxation for about 15 seconds, then repeat the previous steps with other muscle groups until you finish all of them.

14. Once you are done, remain in your position for a few minutes and enjoy feeling completely relaxed.

This exercise can feel uncomfortable at first, but in time, it will be enjoyable.

N.B.: You should only experience tension in your muscles. If you feel intense pain, you are doing something wrong, so stop right away. Be gentle while practicing this exercise, and don't hurt yourself.

If you have medical issues, broken bones, or pulled muscles, speak to your doctor before you practice this technique.

Yoga

Yoga relaxes the muscles, reduces stress, and increases blood flow.
https://unsplash.com/photos/F2qh3yjz6Jk

Yoga involves physical and mental exercises that can soothe your mind and relax your body. Practice yoga rather than scrolling on your phone or watching TV before bed. It relaxes the muscles, reduces stress, and increases blood flow.

Instructions:

1. Sit up straight in a cross-legged position on the floor. Make sure you are comfortable. If you aren't, sit on a yoga mat or a cushion.

2. Place your left hand on your left knee and your right hand on your right knee.

3. Close your eyes.

4. Let go of all your stress, and don't think of the past or worry about the future. You are only in the here and now.

5. Take a few long breaths and notice how your body feels with every breath.

Meditation

If you suffer from anxiety or have trouble sleeping, meditation is the best remedy. It quietens your mind and prepares your body for sleep.

Instructions:

1. Find a quiet room with no distractions.

2. Shut the blinds and turn off the lights.

3. Sit in a comfortable position or lie down if you prefer.

4. Close your eyes and breathe in slowly through your nostrils and out through your mouth. Focus only on your breathing. Feel your chest rising and falling with every breath.

5. Scan every part of your body, from your feet to your head. If a body part feels comfortable, hold on to this feeling, but if you experience any tension, release it by breathing out and imagining the tension sinking into the ground.

6. Now, visualize that you are in a place that makes you feel happy and at peace. This can be a real place you have been to or wish to go to one day, a beautiful memory that puts a smile on your face, or an imaginary place.

7. Take in everything about your surroundings, and don't allow intrusive thoughts to ruin the moment.

8. Repeat any simple mantras to signal to your brain to relax, like *"I am calm and at peace."*

9. It's normal for your mind to wander and for intrusive thoughts to creep in. Let them pass and bring your thoughts to your breathing and the beautiful image you are visualizing.

10. Don't ask yourself, "Am I feeling relaxed?" Or "Will I sleep well at night?" These questions will only bring self-doubt. Just enjoy the experience.

Create a Pre-Sleep Ritual

You can have a ritual every night before bed where you mentally call out your power animal through visualization techniques. Visualization is a mental exercise that you do while meditating. It involves picturing in detail a specific experience you want to live, or in this case, meeting your power animal.

Instructions:

1. Find a quiet room and sit in a comfortable position.
2. Close your eyes and take a few long and deep breaths.
3. Inhale through your nostrils, hold your breath for as long as possible, and exhale through your mouth.
4. Clear your thoughts and only focus on your power animal.
5. Set an intention by saying something like, "*I am calling on my power animal to come to me in my dreams.*"
6. By now, you should have identified your power animal so it will be easy to visualize it and establish a connection with it.
7. Mentally invite your power animal to come to you in your dreams.
8. Before you sleep, keep your mind and heart open to the idea that you will meet your power animal in your dreams.

Repeat this visualization technique every night until you dream about your power animal.

Dream Incubation

The concept of dream incubation is quite similar to the plot of the movie Inception.
https://unsplash.com/photos/902vnYeoWS4

Dream incubation is planting the person, idea, place, situation, etc., in your mind that you want to see in your dreams. Does this sound familiar? The concept of dream incubation is quite similar to the plot of the movie Inception. However, in this scenario, you won't have to experience a dream within a dream; just one will suffice.

In dream incubation, you focus on your power animal every night before you go to sleep. According to neuroscientist Sidarta Ribeiro, some cultures, like the Native Americans, believe they are in control of their dreams, not the other way around. You don't only choose who you want to dream about but also the plot, location, theme, and everything else in the dream.

Instructions:

1. Set an intention for the dream incubation, like, *"I will dream about my power animal,"* and repeat it to yourself.

2. Associate the words you choose for your intention with an emotion like love or joy so that when you say them, you also experience the emotion.

3. Repeat these words all day, not just before bed. You can say them out loud or under your breath or simply think of them and the emotions you associate with them. The more you repeat your intention, the higher your chances of dreaming about your power animal.

4. Write the intention on a piece of paper and put it under the pillow.

5. Before you sleep at night, visualize seeing your power animal in your dreams. Imagine any scenario you like and try to make it real. Imagine all the details, such as what your power animal looks like, what you will be wearing, what you will both be doing, and what you will say to each other.

6. Add as many details as possible, like the emotions you will feel when you see your power animal, their scent, voice, and touch.

7. You can also visualize waking up the next morning after seeing the dream. Imagine feeling happy and excited about meeting your power animal.

8. You can try other things besides visualization to incubate a dream. For instance, you can look at pictures of your power animal (the animal it represents), talk about it or write about it in

your journal, imagine it guiding or protecting you, or draw a picture of it. While doing any of these things, mentally ask your power animal to meet you in your dreams.

9. Before you go to sleep, put a picture of your power animal under your pillow or wear its symbol as a pendant around your neck.

10. You can also repeat your intention while practicing any of the relaxation techniques in this chapter. Relaxation techniques can greatly impact dream incubation as your subconscious mind is more receptive to ideas when your brain is relaxed.

11. As you close your eyes to fall asleep, ask your unconscious mind to remember your dream.

12. Keep repeating the intentions, experiencing the emotions, and seeing the visualization until you fall asleep. Imagine they are seeds, and you are planting them in your unconscious mind.

13. When you wake up, write down everything you saw in your dream before you forget. If you see your power animal, write what happened in detail and include your conversation and everything you experienced. There could be a message here somewhere.

14. Believe that this technique will work. If you have any doubts, this can impact the process, and you might be unable to remember your dream.

Associating your dreams with an emotion is necessary for this technique to work. If you think of any of the dreams you had throughout your life, you will notice that certain emotions influenced them. For instance, when you are afraid, you dream of someone chasing you. Or when you are experiencing anxiety, you dream of taking an exam. Emotions are the most significant dream trigger and will strengthen your intention so it can influence your subconscious.

Don't be discouraged if you don't dream about your power animal right away. This process can take a few days or more. For some people, it takes them a long time to master the skill of dream incubation, so be patient with yourself. Or perhaps your power animal feels you aren't ready to meet yet. However, repeat the process every day, and don't give up, as it can happen when you least expect it.

Lucid Dreams

Lucid dreams are different from dream incubation. Dream incubation is a process that influences your dream while you are still awake, while lucid dreaming is becoming aware that you are dreaming when you're asleep.

When people mention lucid dreams, the first thought that usually comes to mind is dream control. However, these two are also different. In lucid dreams, you become aware that you aren't awake. Dream control usually comes after this realization. In other words, once you notice you are dreaming, you can then take control of your dream. However, you may also choose to let the events play out and not interfere. Either way, it's your choice.

If you can achieve lucid dreams, you can invite your power animal to come to you while dreaming. Or if you dream about them, you can become aware that you are dreaming and control the scenario.

There are certain things that you can do to experience lucid dreams.

Keep a Dream Journal

Achieving lucid dreaming requires you to become aware of your innermost thoughts. Keep a dream journal next to your bed and write down your dreams after you wake up before you forget them. This will increase your self-awareness, which is necessary to achieve lucid dreaming. Even if you don't remember your whole dream, just write down whatever comes to mind.

If you don't feel like writing when you wake up in the morning, you can use a voice-recording app. You can also draw images if you prefer that over writing. Choose any method you want as long as you record your dreams every morning. Look at your journal daily and study your common dream patterns.

Daily Reality Checks

Reality checks are a technique you can practice throughout the day to test if you are asleep or awake. This will teach you the difference between your waking life and your dreams. Reality checks include simple things you can practice while working or studying.

- Pinch yourself. If you don't feel anything, you are dreaming.
- Look in the mirror. If you see something strange, you are dreaming.

- Check the time once, then look away and check again. In dreams, every time you look at the clock, the time changes, and the hands of the clock usually don't move.
- Press your index finger to check if it is solid or not.
- Pinch your nose and try to breathe. If you breathe normally, you are dreaming.

When you constantly do reality checks while you are awake, your brain will get used to them, and you will do them while dreaming. Once you recognize you are dreaming, you can take control of your dream.

Experiment with the Mild Technique

Mnemonic induction of lucid dreams (MILD) may sound complicated, but the idea here is to set an intention to remember your dreams. When you wake up, spend a couple of minutes thinking of your dream and ask yourself, "Which part of it made it clear that I wasn't awake?" Perhaps the sky was red, zombies haunted you, or you were best friends with Taylor Swift. In other words, pick the unrealistic parts that stood out in the dream.

Then, write in your dream journal what you would have done if you became aware you were dreaming. Include your power animal in this scenario, and let your imagination run wild. Perhaps you can bring it into the dream scenario to go on a journey together or ask it for guidance and seek its wisdom.

Tell yourself that you will recognize that you are dreaming next time.

The Way Back to Bed Technique

Lucid dreaming occurs during REM (Rapid Eye Movement) sleep. The way back to bed technique tricks your brain to stay active during REM sleep. Set your alarm to wake you up five hours after you fall asleep. Get out of bed and do something mentally stimulating like playing a puzzle, spotting the difference game on your phone, meditating, or reading. Do this for twenty minutes or more if you can. When you go to sleep, your conscious mind will still be active, and you can experience lucid dreaming.

It takes time to master the skill of lucid dreaming. Keep practicing any or all these exercises every day, and eventually, you will get there.

Affirmations

Affirmations are positive phrases you repeat to yourself daily and can change your thoughts. When you repeatedly say certain words to yourself, your mind will believe these statements must be true.

Repeat affirmations with focused intention about meeting your power animal in your dreams until your brain makes it a reality.

- I want to meet my power animal during my sleep.
- I will see my power animal tonight in my dreams.
- I am in control of my dreams, and I will bring my power animal into them.
- I will ask my power animal for guidance when I meet it in my dreams.
- Tonight, my power animal and I will meet in the dream realm.
- I am ready to meet my power animal in my dreams.

Meeting your power animal in your dream will take time and will require practicing certain skills. Understand that this isn't a marathon, so be patient and believe that you will eventually meet, no matter how long it takes.

Chapter 8: Enhancing Intuitive Communication

Have you ever felt envious of people who make decisions at a moment's notice, simply trusting that everything will turn out okay? They go with the flow and listen to whatever their gut tells them to do. The same ability could make a vast difference in forming a relationship with your power animal. The key to developing it is honing your intuition, the internal compass that'll keep you on the right path regardless of your choices or obstacles in your way. Any messages you receive from your power animal will register in your subconscious. To access and decipher them, you need a gateway between your subconscious and conscious - and this is where your intuition comes in. When you tap into it, you access your subconscious thoughts and emotions.

Trusting your gut isn't easy, especially regarding spiritual messages. There are so many preconceived notions, prejudices, and biases surrounding spiritual communication, not to mention all that chatter going on about day-to-day issues in your head. To tap into and listen to your intuition, you must learn to shut out external stimuli and your ego. The latter is the part that always wants more and never feels like it has enough. When communicating with your power animal, less is often more.

Moreover, when trying to work with one's inner wisdom, an added challenge is learning to distinguish between the voice of fear and the representative of clear perception. However, the more you trust your intuition and follow the messages from your power animal, the more you can rely on your gut. This chapter brings you plenty of tips and practical exercises for enhancing your intuitive communication skills to achieve this.

Animal Yoga Poses (Asanas)

The Full Pranam

Instructions:

1. Start by lying down on your mat, face down.

2. Extend your arms in front of you, palms facing up.

3. Lay down your forehead on the mat.

4. Take 5-10 deep breaths. While you do, mentally dispel the part of yourself driven by pride. It blocks spiritual communication and silences your intuition.

The Humble Warrior

Instructions:

1. Stand with your feet a hip's width apart and place one foot forward.

2. Press your heel down. Your toes should face the mat's top corner. (For example, if you move your left foot back, the toes on this foot will point toward the mat's top left corner).

3. Lift your arms and move your hands towards your back. When they touch, move your front foot farther toward the side of the mat.

4. Take a deep breath and lift your chest upward. As you exhale, move your torso downward and toward the inner side of your front leg.

5. Release any strain from your neck and let your head hang heavily. Your hips will not be perfectly parallel with the mat top, and that's all right.

6. Hold the pose for five breaths and switch sides.

Alternate Breathing

Instructions:

1. Find a comfortable position, take a deep breath, and close your eyes.

2. Palms up, place your left hand on your left thigh. Your index finger should be touching your palm.

3. Place your right hand's index and middle finger between your eyebrows (on your third eye).

4. Place your thumb on your right nostril and draw in a deep breath through the open left nostril while counting to six.

Place your thumb on your right nostril and draw in a deep breath through the open left nostril while counting to six.

5. Then, block your left nostril with your ring finger. Release your breath through your other nostril while counting to six.

6. Pause and take a deep breath through the same nostril while counting to six.

7. Then, close the right nostril with your thumb and release your breath through your left nostril while counting to six.

8. Repeat steps four to seven times.

Meditations for Deepening and Strengthening the Bond with Your Power Animal

Aligning Your Energies with Meditation and Prayer

Whether you have trouble defining a problem you need help with or focusing on your intention, it can hinder your ability to reach out to your power animal. A short meditation session can help you regain focus and discover what you need help with. It will also allow you to align your spiritual energy with the energy of the power animal.

Instructions:

1. Start by finding a quiet space where you won't be disturbed.

2. Turn your focus away from your conscious thoughts - so your mind isn't occupied with worries and to-do lists.

3. Then, start focusing on your breath. Take a few deep breaths and feel how the air travels through your body. When you feel relaxed, visualize a warm, golden light enveloping you from all sides.

4. Picture your power animal and feel its energy meeting you through the light around you. Be positive and grateful for the energy that allows you to ask anything you want.

5. Then, proceed to ask your question or make your inquiry. Repeat this simple meditation for 5-20 minutes every day or whenever you feel disconnected from your power animal.

Alternatively, you can also say a prayer, with or without meditation. You can recite one before or after meditative exercises, when sitting at your altar, or anywhere you want to reflect on spiritual communication. Although it doesn't have to be a long prayer, don't forget to give thanks. You can say something like this:

"Thank you, my friend, for illuminating my path and showing me what to do regarding (insert the issues you asked assistance for).

I ask you to keep me on the right path

And I thank you for whatever gifts you bestow upon me."

Divinations Tools for Receiving Messages and Insights

Do your practices involve drawing cards or similar divination forms? If yes, you can use them alongside visualization to retrieve your power animal or at least ask them to send you signs of their presence and willingness to help.

There are several divination tools you can use for spiritual communication. Tarot cards, Oracle cards, and Norse runes are some of the most popular methods. Each offers a simple way to contact your power animal and ask for an answer, assistance, alignment, or whatever you need to reach your future goals. The tools you use will serve as conductors for the messages flowing back and forth between you and your power animal. If you've never used divination tools before, you might want to try several of them to see which ones suit your spiritual energy. You can make your inquiry as simple or as complex as you want.

Instructions:

1. For starters, ask a simple question by holding one object in your hand (a card, rune, or another tool).
2. Close your eyes and focus on the energy surrounding the object in your hands while taking a few deep, relaxing breaths.
3. After centering yourself, ask your power animal for their assistance, and open your mind to the answers you'll receive.

Or:

1. Ask for a sign from your animal before drawing a card, and try to visualize the message you receive through the card. Depending on how specific your questions or needs are, the answers will differ.
2. If you need an immediate resolution, the animal will most certainly appear to you soon in an unmistakable way. However, if you are asking your power animal to accompany you on a particular path, be prepared to encounter it only in the subtle signs around you.

Journaling

Writing to your power animal is another way to contact and nurture your intuitive relationship with them. You can simply write on a piece of paper, or - if you want to make this into a regular habit - get a journal for writing down your thoughts and wishes regarding spiritual help. The latter will allow you to revisit them and track your progress in sharpening your psychic abilities.

Writing to your power animal is another way to contact and nurture your intuitive relationship with them.

https://unsplash.com/photos/3ZvHsFiZyME

Instructions:

1. If you want to use a journal to intuitively meet your power animal, start with an invitation and expression of gratitude, like the following one:

    "Thank you, my friend, for revealing the wisdom you wanted me to have. I welcome you to come to me."

2. Then, take a deep breath and let your thoughts flow. Write them as they come - whether they're random ideas, visions, short or long stories, or anything you haven't thought of before - it doesn't matter. They might all contain a message your power animal wants you to have. So don't second guess anything. Just record everything.

3. Your power animal might also choose to speak directly to you while you're in the process of writing.

4. Initially, write in the first person. Have you noticed that you've suddenly switched to the second person? If yes, it might be your power animal that's writing these lines. You might also see your handwriting change drastically when they take over.

5. After you're done, read over what you've written and try to interpret their message by tapping into your intuition.

Sharpening Sensory Awareness

If your schedule allows it, visit the nearest natural area to bring yourself closer to the spirit of your animal and help it appear sooner. When you find this secluded place, sit quietly and listen to the sounds of nature. Pay attention to the smells and the colors, and hone in on anything that catches your attention.

Nature can be an incredibly versatile instrument for spiritual communication. Building a profound connection with nature will give you access to its powers whenever you need them for grounding, healing, or reaching out to the spiritual realm. All it takes is spending a few minutes a day in nature (even standing on your balcony surrounded by potted plants counts), and allowing it to ground you will give you the sense of tranquility and empowerment you need. Taking regular long walks in nature or stopping and meditating within its energies and using it for healing exercises will provide you with even more benefits for your budding intuitive practices.

Honing Your Instincts

An innate affinity with a particular animal might be a clue that they are your power animal. If there is an animal you have been fascinated with for a long time since a long time ago, regularly drew as a child, or saw in your dreams, you might have been instinctively communicating with your power animal all along. This is particularly true if you have never seen the animal in real life. However, it could also mean you were already noticing signs of it around you without being aware of it - but you picked up the clues with your intuition. They have been preparing you subconsciously, so when the time comes for them to enter your life, you can accept them consciously as well. Sound familiar? If yes, your gut tells you always had a friend when you needed one. Start listening to it instinctively. Now that you are ready to embrace the full symbolism of your power animal, all you need to do is keep honing your instincts. They will lead you to the animal that will teach you how to embrace their power and your own. Wherever you notice a message or a sign in an unusual place, ask yourself, "Is this my power animal speaking to me"?

Challenges or Obstacles of Working with Your Power Animal and How to Overcome Them

As dreadful as they seem, the challenges you encounter might be opportunities for spiritual growth. Intuition is key to changing your mind from seeing life's hurdles as learning prospects instead of something holding you back.

You're Not Spending Enough Time with Your Power Animal

You can't establish a good rapport with your power animal if you don't spend enough time with them. Consequently, trust and care will be non-existent in your relationship. Show your consideration for the life and home of your power animal. Don't engage in behavior that could destroy their natural habitat. Another way to show respect for your power animal is by wearing a pendant or a piece of clothing that displays their image. Let this image keep you conscious of and open to the animal's guidance.

Occasionally, you'll want to show appreciation for your power animal. This will keep your relationship strong. Apart from thanking them for the blessings they send your way, you'll also want to give thanks for any opportunities and assignments that have helped your spiritual development. You might find these challenging at times, but it's critical to let the spirits know you're grateful for them – and that they're welcome to send more wisdom on your way.

Whether you do it at your altar, during a gathering, or any other way, making an offering can be a respectful way to show appreciation towards your power animal. The offering doesn't even have to be a physical item. Surrendering a piece of information about yourself works just as well. Your spiritual allies won't mind even if you do it to vent or give yourself a break. It's like getting to know a friend. They want to know how to help you, - and by offering something about yourself, - you are giving them a tool to do so. They'll also be grateful because they know that your offering is a show of trust.

You're Not Listening to Your Power Animal

If you aren't listening to your power animal, you won't know what they're trying to communicate. Sometimes, their messages might sound silly or hard to believe because you aren't prepared to hear them. Don't make the mistake of ignoring this information, as you might regret it later. For example, a seemingly senseless message might warn of impending danger. Or you might feel drawn to an action, person, or location - but you don't see why you should pursue this impulse. It could be your power animal letting you know about an opportunity you should seize. Failing to listen or contradict their guidance is disrespectful and could make them feel you don't want their help. After all, who would want to keep assisting a friend who refuses to listen to advice?

You Don't Know Your Power Animal

A major hindrance in intuitive communication is not knowing enough about them. Without at least a rudimentary understanding of their likes and dislikes, you can't even dream of developing a profound connection with your power animal. Do your research, and feel free to inquire about them when you meet them.

Here are some questions to ask your power animal to get to know them better:

- What does the animal like to munch on?
- Does this animal make a sound?
- Does this animal have unusual habits (for example, hunting, mating, etc.)?
- Does this animal look the same all the time?
- Where does this animal like to hang out?

Additional Tips

Trusting your intuition is perhaps probably the most challenging task you'll ever face on your journey of bonding with your power animal.

Trusting your intuition is perhaps probably the most challenging task you'll ever face on your journey of bonding with your power animal. You'll need to fully believe that your gift will allow you to call on your power animal and interpret its messages. So, if you have trouble with spiritual communication, you should look into yourself to see why. Do you trust your instincts - your gateway to your psychic gifts? If not, practice them through simple exercises until you become confident in your abilities. The more you practice this, the more frequently you'll be able to receive spiritual messages and allow them to guide you through the journey of life. Your gifts and the wisdom you receive can be helpful to others as well.

You'll also learn to trust your power animal. While many practitioners go above and beyond to encourage their companions to trust them, they still have trouble returning the sentiment. Your bond will never be strong enough if you doubt their ability to guide you. Remember, power animals possess a higher knowledge. They are aware of plans and fates you don't know of, and the ones willing to become your allies are there to protect, guide, and love you. Don't try to control the situation by focusing on the outcome you want them to lead you towards. Let them decide, and you won't regret it.

Another tip to make establishing spiritual communication easier is to ground yourself afterward. Spiritual energy is empowering, but the energy shift you feel when receiving a message can be unsettling. It can prevent you from interpreting the information correctly and make you fearful of the next session. To avoid this, perform a quick grounding exercise after each session. You can do this by taking off your shoes and feeling the ground with the soles of your feet, sitting on a rock in the park, or simply finding a patch of nature and taking in its stillness. You can do anything that works as a reminder of your presence in this world and your human experiences.

Chapter 9: The Animal Medicine Wheel

Power and totem animals can be powerful allies used for healing in various spiritual and Shamanic practices, addressing physical, emotional, mental, and spiritual imbalances. This chapter explores the sacred and spiritual concept of the animal medicine wheel and its use in spiritual practices.

What Is a Medicine Wheel?

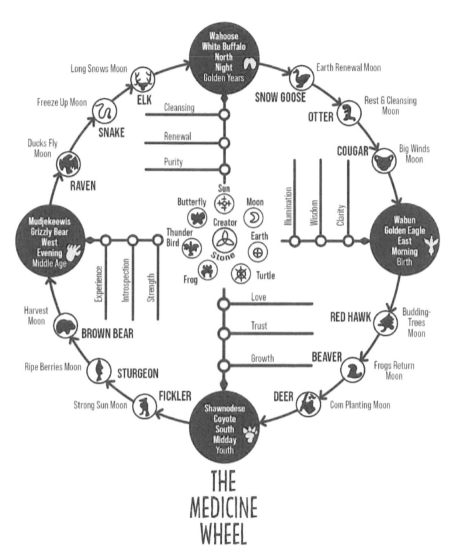

The medicine wheel is a symbol rooted in ancient practices of indigenous cultures.

The medicine wheel is a symbol rooted in ancient practices of indigenous cultures. For them, the meaning of life takes a circular form. Hence, the same shape is used for medicine wheels. Moreover, it signifies the interconnectedness of all creatures and non-living aspects of the natural world. In some cultures, the structure is called a sacred circle or sacred hoop. While they can contain different elements, what most medicine wheels have in common is being divided into four quadrants. The number four is sacred to cultures from where the symbol originates. Each quadrant is associated with fundamental qualities of life.

In other cultures, the medicine wheel is said to hold vast knowledge of the universe. According to a third interpretation, it signifies hope and the possibility of harnessing healing powers for those who seek it.

Did you know some ancient medicine wheels are estimated to be millions of years old? The oldest one that has been dated was created around 4000 B.C., but much older ones exist, and their dates cannot be confirmed. The term "Medicine Wheel" is much younger and was coined by non-indigenous practitioners at the turn of the last century.

Besides the classic stone medicine wheels, other popular depictions include a simple (often painted or printed on paper) circle divided into four differently colored parts. The black, white, red, and yellow quadrants are often featured in art, on instruments, and other tools associated with indigenous or Shamanic practices. More detailed illustrations include the green inner circle (center). The order of the colors within the circle is particular to each culture, as are the attributes they represent.

The Key Elements of a Medicine Wheel

Each medicine wheel has several crucial elements. These include the circle, the four directions, and the lines. When building a simple wheel, the latter can be omitted, but they should still be acknowledged when setting an intention or connecting to the wheel's powers.

The Circle

The circle of the medicine wheel signifies the outer boundary of life on the earthly plain or nature itself. Besides the continuous cycle of life and death, the circle represents numerous ideas featured in ancient indigenous cultures. Some tied it to the phases of the moon and the sun's path, while others associated it with the sacred circle of the home, shielding those residing in it. According to another belief, the circle is tied to the creator, who made it possible for life and the natural world to grow and evolve. Cultures centering on this belief affirm that every force on earth works together, is connected, and continuously moves toward its destiny. They see everything happening around them as part of the natural cycle. Based on yet another belief, the power of the circle lies in its ability to separate and connect at the same time. It claims that when you merge your energy with the circle, you have nothing standing in your way or holding you back from behind — yet you're intertwined with the entire natural world.

Medicine wheels come in different forms and sizes, and their meaning and use are culture-specific. However, there is a fundamental similarity in all cultures. Medicine wheels denote the perfect alignment and interaction of life's physical, spiritual, emotional, and mental facets. The circle, in essence, represents the core — the awareness of oneself and the knowledge to empower oneself to grow and take charge of one's life.

The Lines

Most medicine wheels have vertical and horizontal lines (even if invisible, as in not represented in the wheel's structure or picture), symbolizing peoples' and the sun's path. The lines intercept each other in the middle of the circle, denoting the interconnectedness of people's lives with the sun's path and the significance of this connection on people's lives.

Correspondences of the Wheel

The correspondences of the wheel vary just as much as their significance in the different cultures. However, the four quadrants often have similar meanings.

The Four Directions

The medicine wheel's quadrants denote the four directions: east, west, north, and south. Participants start with the east quadrant and move clockwise around the wheel when addressing or connecting to the directions. If you see a four-colored medicine wheel, red denotes the south, yellow the east, white the north, and black the west.

The Four Seasons

The four seasons are also symbolized in the medicine wheel's quadrants.
https://unsplash.com/photos/5IHz5WhosQE

The four seasons (winter, spring, summer, and fall) are also symbolized in the medicine wheel's quadrants. When connecting to the wheel, practitioners start with the spring quadrant — the same way life begins anew in spring after dying in winter. It's a time of birth and rebirth. The quadrant representing summer brings an abundance of fresh food, ready to be harvested, along with the fruits of your labor. The quadrant belonging to fall equates to maturation. It's the time of harvest. The winter's quadrant denotes death and the completion of life's cycle.

The Four Elements

The four elements, earth, fire, wind, and water, might also be attributed to the four quadrants of the medicine wheel. One quadrant represents fire, from which you obtain warmth and light for healing. The next quadrant belongs to the earth, where you gain sustenance and the wonders of natural medicine — it's closely tied to life. The quadrant denoting water holds essential energies to your body and the body of all creatures on earth. The last quadrant symbolizes wind and is the invisible force spreading life in its wake.

The Animal Medicine Wheel

Animal spirits represent the energies and attributes associated with each direction. Regarding animal medicine wheels, there is no limit or rule on which creatures can be associated with the wheel or quadrants they govern. Various ancient cultures attributed different animals to different parts of the wheel, leaving contemporary practitioners with many choices. As a beginner, you can look into the common spirit animals often associated with the wheel, including the bear, the eagle, the coyote, and the buffalo.

Associated with the eastern quadrant, the eagle denotes keen vision. You'll resort to this section if you have trouble seeing the big picture. Its power widens your perspectives, removing the limitations of earth-bound ideas and views. In some cultures, the eagle is a messenger animal, carrying missives between the heavenly and earthly realms. In others, this magnificent bird is a spiritual protector — watching you from above in the sky. The eagle can give you strength and wisdom in spiritual challenges.

The spirit guard of the northern quadrant, the buffalo, is the personification of psychical strengths, endurance, and courage. The animal will empower you emotionally by making you feel stronger physically. The buffalo signifies abundance, power, solidness, and groundedness in other cultures. If you need centering and reinforcing your connection to nature, the buffalo is a fantastic aid to call on.

In other cultures, the northern quadrant is linked to the bear, the king of the forest animals. Given its tendency to walk on two legs, some tribes view the bear as a brother to people. The bear is a source of strength and confidence, two critical elements of healing both emotional and physical traumas. Some cultures associate the bear with the western quadrant. They see the bear as a furious totem animal, often leading with aloofness. If you need to take command of your situation to heal, this is the animal to turn to. The bear might also symbolize the need for solitary reflection. It might prompt you to rely on your individual forces to fuel your courage instead of relying on others.

In some cases, the northern quadrant is tied to the rabbit or the mouse, animals known for their diligent work. They might be smaller than a buffalo or bear, but they can be just as powerful allies when you work toward a bigger goal by achieving smaller ones first.

In other cultures, the mouse embodies persistence and is the spirit keeper of the northern quadrant. Unlike the eagle, the mouse prompts you to pay attention to tiny details. If you need to determine which facts will be useful for your healing journey and which won't, call on the mouse in the southern quadrant. It will increase your awareness and enable you to sacrifice your ego if necessary. After all, when have you seen a mouse survive on anything other than meager scraps? It can teach you a powerful lesson.

The coyote, a playful but cunning animal known for its unusual wisdom, can also govern the southern quadrant. It can be a great aid when you need lighthearted energy for emotional healing. According to another belief, the coyote teaches the lessons of trusting your gut and freeing yourself from unnecessary burdens.

The hawk has been associated with different parts of the medicine wheel. However, in all cultures, this bird is seen as a messenger and the source of sharp focus. By making you observant at the right times, it can help you overcome stressful situations. It shows that sometimes it's better to stop and listen than to despair.

Also belonging to various quadrants across different cultures, the elk is associated with the power of letting go. Slow and steady wins the race - by paying attention to your basic needs instead of chasing your goals, you'll get much closer to your target. The elk can also teach you about the importance of long-term plans versus quick results.

Like the elk, the deer might also guide different parts of the medicine wheel. This totem animal is linked to gentleness and compassion — motivating you to create a healing environment for yourself or others. It's about finding a balance between your emotional and physical needs. In some cultures, the deer is seen as one of the purest animals, capable of traveling between realism and carrying spiritual messages. Its quiet strengths allow it to deliver messages lovingly, regardless of their content.

Known for its power of transmutation, the snake is the spirit keeper of the southern quadrant in certain cultures. It possesses lessons of birth and transforming negative energies into positive ones. If you struggle with adapting to negative circumstances, the snake will empower you to move forward through purification. Be prepared. Just like the animal, the totem acts quickly and without warning.

Linked to diverse parts of the medicine wheel, the skunk symbolizes reputation. It's the animal power you need to gain respect and honor. However, you must show your true face and abilities (no matter how repellent they might seem). They'll only repel those whose values don't align with yours when you want to attract like-minded people.

The moose is another animal tied to more than one part of the wheel. It's a symbol of wisdom, the totem you need to share your knowledge and teach others the art of healing. In some cultures, this animal's energy can be useful for preparing oneself for spiritual journeys.

How to Build an Animal Medicine Wheel

Since there are no strict rules on building a medicine wheel, you can make it as simple or as elaborate as you want. If you're just dipping your toes into the practice, you might feel more comfortable making a simple structure from a handful of stones, like the one described below. It has suggestions for which animals to call on in each direction, but you can substitute them with others. Five rocks or crystals in a circle while calling to spirit guardians of each part is all you need.

Five rocks or crystals in a circle while calling to spirit guardians of each part is all you need.
https://unsplash.com/photos/qayNP9ccw9E

Instructions:

1. Place a stone to represent the east. In most cases, this direction is guarded by the eagle and will be associated with mental clarity. As you do, focus on an intention aligned with this facet. Have you ever seen an eagle circling the sky while searching for prey on a field? Use the same approach when establishing your intention — browsing through a field of mental pictures until you find the right one.

2. Moving clockwise, repeat the process for the remaining directions. As you place the stone for the south, formulate the intention aligning with the spirit guardian's power. For example, for the coyote, it will be spiritual well-being. Whereas for a

serpent, it's finding your identity or purpose.

3. Placing a stone to represent the West, you can base your intention on the bear's power and the hidden emotions or unwanted memories it represents. For the north, you'll likely be aligning your power with the buffalo and its immense source of physical empowerment.

4. When you complete your stone circle, channel your focus to its center. Place the remaining stone in the middle of the circle to honor the creator and the unification of all powers within the wheel.

The beauty of a small animal medicine wheel is that you set them up anywhere and remove them when necessary. If you feel a strong affinity to nature, set up your wheel in your garden to be even closer to nature's power. You'll have a peaceful, healing space to stand or sit in. Even if you (or anyone else in your household) only walk by as you tend to your garden, you'll still feel its benefits.

Alternatively, if your practice includes building an altar, you can set up your animal medicine wheel at this sacred place. This could be a great way to honor its spirit guides, as the altar will help you channel your intention or enhance the power of the gifts you'll receive.

Whichever place you choose to build your animal medicine wheel, visit it regularly to better understand its powers. Another idea is to design a separate wheel for every member of your household. It will empower their healing and boost their well-being to avoid future health issues. Naturally, you'll need to ask their permission before you channel any energy towards them, no matter how natural and healing it might be.

How to Connect to Your Wheel

By connecting with an animal medicine wheel, you can identify areas of imbalance and work with the medicine wheel's healing energy. The correspondences of animals and attributes vary among different cultures. Still, it's a good idea to approach the practice of implementing the animal medicine wheel with respect and sensitivity to its origins and traditional background.

When you need spiritual guidance, go to your animal medicine wheel and channel your intention to connect to it.

Here is how to do it:

1. Walking around the wheel's circle counter-clockwise to reinforce your focus on your intention. Start from the east and complete the circle three times (if you feel that you need more clarity, do more laps).

2. As you walk, focus on your breathing, the circle, and its natural power. Finish your laps at the east point.

3. Call on the spirit guide of the east (whichever animal you determined on your wheel), asking for their permission to harness the power of the medicine wheel. It helps dispel low vibrational energies from your energy field, and asking for it shows you're respecting the animals and nature (the same way you appreciate someone asking to use something yours).

4. You'll know you can proceed when you don't feel any resistance in energy when reaching out to the wheel. Then, light a candle and use the fire from the candle to light a smudge stick. Smudge yourself before you fully connect to the wheel so no residual negativity will be left within or around you.

5. Stand to the left side of the eastmost stone. Take a slow, deep breath and release it. As you do, say your intention to use the wheel. Be as specific as possible (saying what part of the wheel's medicine/power you want to connect to) and use your full birth name instead of saying, *"I."*

6. Walk clockwise around the wheel and focus on connecting to the wheel. Start and stop at east and express your gratitude for the knowledge or blessings you're about to receive, for there will be plenty. You can do this by simply saying thanks or reciting a prayer of your choice. Alternatively, you can thank the wheel in the name of others if you're planning to use the wheel's powers for their benefit later on.

You have several options if you wish to connect to different parts of the wheel. Choose whichever way you feel comfortable with the most. One of the ways is to connect to the parts you want to learn about or use separately. If you choose this option, simply sit in the direction representing that part and listen to its guidance. The other way is to connect to the spirit guide of the East and then reach out to the part you want to learn about or use. For example, after connecting to the east, turn toward the north and call in the spirit guide of the north. This is great for beginners because no matter where you are, you can evoke the guardian of a direction and feel its power enveloping you.

Chapter 10: Power Animal Wisdom in Daily Life

By now, you've learned how to connect with your spirit animals in more ways than one. Whether it's through meditation, yoga, or a Shamanic journey, these animals always come to your rescue when called upon. You can call on your power animals to help you when you're facing a particular challenge, connecting to totems with certain attributes that prove helpful for specific situations. However, you don't have to wait until you're faced with a certain problem to call on your power animal, or any power animal for that matter. In fact, it's better to connect to different power animals daily. You'll be surprised at how many different ways power animals can help you, whether you're nervous for a job interview, need confidence for a date, or simply seek comfort after a sad day. When you practice this daily, you can cultivate a deeper bond with the natural world and your inner self. This consistent interaction with various totems allows you to tap into a diverse range of qualities and energies, which helps you navigate the complexity of daily life with more grace and resilience.

Imagine starting your morning with a short meditation, inviting a specific power animal to be with you throughout the day. Maybe you call on the owl's wisdom to help you approach challenges with insight and clarity. As you go about your day, you may find that you can see situations from a different perspective and are making better decisions as a result. In the afternoon, you might shift gears and connect with a cheetah's swift and agile energy. This choice can infuse you with a burst of energy and determination, which can help you tackle tasks that require speed and precision. You might find yourself completing tasks more efficiently. As the evening settles in, you could call on a bear's calm and nurturing presence. This totem helps you unwind, release stress, and find comfort in your own solitude. Connecting with the bear can promote self-care and rejuvenation, preparing you for a restful night's sleep. This is just one example of what you can do to incorporate power animals into your routine. There are so many combinations and possibilities that you can try a different one every day for a long while.

The beauty of connecting with your power animals daily is that it helps you become more flexible. Each animal has its own strengths and qualities you can use whenever you need them. Practicing this connection encourages you to discover different parts of who you are and teaches you how to handle all kinds of situations in life. As time passes, you'll feel even closer to these spirit animals. You might start to sense their presence even when you're not meditating. Sometimes, you'll notice signs and symbols related to these animals that remind you of the good energy you're getting from them. So, whether you're facing something really nerve-wracking, trying to make a tough choice, or just wanting some positive energy in your day, your power animals have your back.

Daily Meditations

Meditation helps you take a break from your busy life and take a moment for your mind.

Meditation helps you take a break from your busy life and take a moment for your mind. It helps you relax, clear your thoughts, and feel better. Some people believe that meditating with your power animal can make your meditative state even deeper. Incorporate this meditation into your daily routine, either when starting the day or before you go to bed, calling on your power animals. Usually, it's suggested that you sit down, but if you want, you can lie down too. If you lie down, lift one of your forearms up at a 90-degree angle to keep yourself from falling asleep completely. This way, if you doze off, your forearm will fall down and wake you up.

When you practice this meditation, you'll go to a special plane called the lower world. It's not what you normally would think of as the underworld—it's an etheric space. People practicing Shamanism believe in this, and it's a safe place to visit. The animal spirits live here. You might meet the animal spirit you were expecting during this journey, but you might not. Even if you have a preferred power animal, a different one might show up. Don't worry, as the animal that appears is the perfect one to help with whatever you're thinking about or feeling.

- Put on some soft, ambient music to create a calming atmosphere. Dim the lights in the room to help create a relaxing environment.
- Sit down in a comfortable chair or cushion. Ensure you're sitting in a relaxed way that doesn't strain your body.
- Begin by taking a couple of slow and deep breaths. Inhale deeply through your nose, and then exhale slowly through your mouth. This helps you relax and calm down.
- When you're ready, gently close your eyes. Letting your eyes rest helps you focus your attention inward.
- As you exhale, let go of any tension or worries you might be feeling. Imagine releasing them with each breath.
- If you have a special spirit animal or any other spiritual beings you connect with, ask them for protection and support during this meditation. Visualize their presence around you.
- Let your attention follow your breath as you breathe naturally. Just observe the rhythm of your breathing for a little while.
- Imagine yourself gently sinking into the Earth's lower world. Picture yourself descending comfortably, knowing you're safe

and protected.

- Pay attention to any physical sensations as you imagine this descent. Feel the sense of sinking or moving downwards.

- As you reach the lower world, visualize yourself landing softly on a grassy meadow. Take a moment to observe the area. Notice the colors, sounds, smells, and sensations around you.

- In front of you, you'll see different paths. You can choose to stay in the meadow or explore further. Think about where you'd like to go and pick a path.

- Walk along the path you've chosen. If you stay in the meadow, find a comfortable place to sit. If you've chosen to explore, walk until you find a comfortable place to sit.

- If you're in the meadow, get comfortable and feel the ground beneath you. If you're at a different location, sit comfortably and take a moment to breathe.

- Reflect on the question or concern you have in mind. Take your time to phrase it clearly in your thoughts.

- Visualize an animal approaching you. This animal is your spirit guide for this meditation. Trust that it's the right one for your question.

- Remember that this animal guide might not be the one you were expecting. It might not be your totem or power animal. That's okay. Trust that it's the right guide for your purpose.

- In your mind, send your question to the animal guide. Imagine a telepathic communication where your thoughts are being transmitted to the guide.

- After you've asked your question, watch for the response from your animal guide. The response could come in various forms: images, feelings, sounds, or thoughts.

- Don't try to analyze or interpret the information yet. Just notice what you receive without judgment.

- If the response isn't clear, you can ask your animal guide for further clarification or more information.

- Take a few moments to absorb the guidance you've received. Allow the insights to sink in without rushing to understand them fully.

- Thank your animal spirit guide for their assistance. This could be done mentally or through a sense of appreciation.
- Bid farewell to your animal guide. Thank them once again for their guidance and presence.
- Imagine yourself gently lifting up from the lower world. Visualize yourself rising back to the place where you started the meditation.
- As you imagine the ascent, start wiggling your fingers and toes. This helps you reconnect with your physical body.
- When you're ready, slowly open your eyes. Take a moment to adjust to the light and your surroundings.
- Look around the room and remind yourself of where you are. This helps you transition back to your present reality.
- If you wish, jot down any notes about your meditation experience. This can help you remember the insights and feelings you received.

Tuning in to the Natural World

When talking about animal wisdom, you probably think of wild animals like bobcats, coyotes, eagles, and bears. However, even the animals you see daily or your pets can teach you many things. Just by watching animals and thinking about how they see the world, you can learn to enjoy the present moment more. That's why animals are often important in stories told by Shamans. These stories help you understand the special things each animal can teach you. You can even try using their skills to make your dreams come true.

Imagine seeing a spider making a web in the window, a squirrel hiding its food in the park, or listening to birds talking to each other. These moments can help you connect with nature and what's happening right now. When you pay attention, you might notice patterns or coincidences with animals. If you see a cartoon fox on TV or a small dog that looks like a fox, it can remind you to be as smart as a fox when needed.

You can also learn from animal stories and how they behave.
https://www.pexels.com/photo/doe-walking-near-path-in-forest-4309369/

You can also learn from animal stories and how they behave. These stories can come to you when you're awake or dreaming. Animals make imaginations go wild, and your imagination is a powerful tool for making yourself feel better and get what you want. So, tune into the natural world through your daily routine. For instance, when you walk in the park, notice how the different animals behave. When you take your dog for a walk, watch how they explore their surroundings. See how they sniff and react to different things. While sitting outside, close your eyes and listen to the different bird sounds. Try to identify each bird by its call. Spend time watching your pet cat or dog. Notice their playful or calm behavior, and see if they're showing you something special. Even in the city, you can see animals. Look out for pigeons on sidewalks or squirrels in trees. Open your window and listen to the sounds of nature. You might hear crickets, frogs, or even owls. The point is there are animals in every part of your life. All you have to do is look, and you'll be connected deeper than ever with your spirit animals.

Rituals

Rituals can help you become more awake and aware of your personal dreams and goals. This can make it easier for you to heal and overcome your addiction to suffering. When you think of rituals, your mind probably goes to those highly complex religious practices shown in movies. Even though those can be great if they're part of your Shamanic journey, you can use simple daily rituals to bring your inner wishes into the real world. There are many ways to do this, and you'll know what's right for you. It could be things like praying, dancing, sitting quietly and thinking, or special ceremonies using your altar or medicine bag. Rituals can help you grow in your practice, wherever you are in your journey. And guess what? You can also bring the wisdom of animals into your rituals. Their strong energy can guide you along the way.

Similarly, there are times when working with animals in a clear and specific way can be really helpful. Sometimes, you can get stuck with just one idea or meaning for an animal. This often comes from your own way of thinking or wanting things to be certain. To break this pattern, work with animals in a real way during rituals. For example, you dream of a whale. Instead of deciding right away what that dream means, you could find a tiny picture or engraving of a whale and keep it with you. Stay curious and open about it. You might also put a photo of a whale tail on your special altar and think about it in your mind without deciding what it means. By working this way, you're allowing the deeper wisdom of animals to show up in your life in ways you might not expect.

Here are some stories of people who incorporated these practices in their daily life, and actually saw positive results:

Mia's Discovery Through Meditation:

Seeking a sense of direction in her life, Mia began a daily meditation routine. In these quiet moments, she found herself drawn to a mental image of a wise owl during her sessions. The owl symbolized wisdom and guidance, helping her reflect on her artistic journey. As Mia incorporated the owl's qualities into her daily life—cultivating patience and keen observation—she noticed a positive shift in her creative process. The owl became a personal symbol, a reminder of the insights she found within herself.

Carlos and the Morning Reflection:

Struggling with the pressures of his career, Carlos decided to start each day with a moment of reflection. During this quiet time, he envisioned walking alongside a bear, a creature embodying strength and resilience. This simple practice helped him approach challenges at work with a clearer mindset. The bear, in his mind, became a metaphor for tapping into his inner strength, providing practical guidance rather than mystical revelations. Carlos found empowerment through this daily ritual, applying its principles to navigate the complexities of his professional life.

Sarah's Healing Rituals:

In the process of recovering from a difficult period, Sarah turned to daily rituals for comfort. Through meditation, journaling, and spending time in nature, she found solace and a sense of connection with the world around her. During one meditation, she envisioned a gentle deer— a symbol of resilience and grace. This image became a source of emotional support for Sarah, encouraging her to approach challenges with a more compassionate mindset. The healing she experienced was a gradual, realistic transformation, where the deer served as a reminder of her own inner strength and resilience.

In conclusion, it can be incredibly powerful when you polish your connection with animal wisdom all through your day. Instead of practicing once in a blue moon, you should incorporate small rituals into your everyday routine for continuous and meaningful engagement with the energy of animals. By observing, reflecting on, and connecting with animals regularly, you build a consistent bond with their wisdom. This consistency allows their qualities to become a natural part of your thoughts and actions, pushing you faster toward healing, insight, and personal growth. Just like any skill, regular practice enhances your connection and amplifies the positive impact of animal wisdom on your journey of self-discovery and transformation.

Bonus: Quick Index

A

Ant: Ants are known for their hard work and cooperation. They can teach you the value of diligence, unity, patience, self-control, sacrifice, loyalty, and honesty.

Alligator: Alligators symbolize retribution, showing that actions have consequences. They also represent creativity, efficiency, hostility, bravery, and power.

Anaconda: Anacondas embody balance and patience. They are seen as powerful creatures that hold wisdom and cunning. Their elusiveness adds to their mystique.

Albatross: Albatrosses are associated with freedom and limitless travel. They bring a sense of sensitivity and thoughtfulness to their interactions.

Antelope: Antelopes are energetic and perceptive animals with keen eyesight. They can encourage you to take risks and remain vigilant. Their actions reflect defensiveness.

Armadillo: Armadillos can teach you about sensitivity and humility. They are trustworthy and calm creatures, often focused on defensive behaviors.

B

Beaver: Beavers display determination and vision in their work. They are inventors and fantasizers, reminding you of the power of persistence.

Buffalo: Buffaloes are seen as divine and strong animals. They represent balance and teach you to be thankful for what you have while standing firm.

Bat: Bats bring a sense of challenge, fear, keen observation, and inner depth. They symbolize illusion and clairvoyance, guiding you to look beyond the surface.

Bear: Bears embody power and bravery. While they can be aggressive, they also hold authority and wisdom. Their solitude speaks of their majestic nature.

Bee: Bees symbolize communication, love, and success. They remind you of the value of hard work, protection, and chastity in your endeavors.

Black Swan: Black Swans are associated with empathy, freedom, and joy. They bring dignity and loyalty, revealing beauty in unexpected situations.

Butterfly: Butterflies represent joy, romance, and transformation. Their spiritual nature brings creativity and peace to those who observe them.

Bluebird: Bluebirds bring flexibility and innovation. They remind you to be kind, thankful, and united in your pursuits, leading to a sense of glory.

Bull: Bulls symbolize fertility, strength, and courage. They are expressive and hasty creatures, often embodying a determined and powerful presence.

C

Cardinal: Cardinals bring cheerfulness and brilliance wherever they go. They are bold and extraordinary, radiating dignity and trust in their actions.

Camel: Camels embody endurance, trust, and commitment. Their determination, humility, and patience teach you the value of lasting qualities.

Cheetah: Cheetahs represent quick thinking, passion, and freedom. Their progress and protective instincts make them agile and powerful creatures.

Cat: Cats are associated with magic, curiosity, and affection. They have keen observational skills and a secretive, supernatural aura.

Cougar: Cougars symbolize patience, observation, and sensuality. They are responsible and dependable creatures, embodying the qualities of a spiritual warrior.

Cuckoo: Cuckoos bring flexibility and love. They also represent fortune and balance, highlighting their shrewd and insightful nature.

Caribou: Caribou are nomads known for their flexibility and sensitivity. They offer guidance and assurance as they navigate various environments.

Crane: Cranes represent isolation, integrity, and endurance. They are self-reliant and wise animals, guiding you with their balanced approach.

Crow: Crows are seen as magical and fearless creatures. They symbolize adaptability, wisdom, and transformation, revealing the beauty of change.

D

Deer: Deer embodies love, generosity, and elegance. They show compassion, caring, and determination in their graceful movements.

Dove: Doves represent purity, gentleness, and devotion. They bring hope, love, and communication, often associated with peace and sacrifice.

Dog: Dogs symbolize loyalty, bravery, and friendship. They offer protection, communication, and patience, showcasing their unwavering devotion.

Dolphin: Dolphins bring harmony, assistance, and strength. They symbolize resurgence and liveliness, embodying a sense of freedom.

Dragon: Dragons symbolize transformation, defense, and magic. They motivate with their authority and strength, embodying a sense of mystery.

Dragonfly: Dragonflies represent transformation and emotional connection. They bring liveliness and flexibility, often associated with illusion.

E

Eagle: Eagles are goal-oriented and focused creatures. They are adventurous and resilient, embodying the qualities of vision, power, and freedom.

Elephant: Elephants embody strength, loyalty, and honor. They carry themselves with pride and dignity, symbolizing confidence and royalty.

Emu: Emus symbolizes flexibility and unity. They are expressive and lively, reminding you of the importance of equality and transit.

Elk: Elks are strong and self-reliant animals. They display cleverness and magnificence, often embodying generosity and dignity.

F

Falcon: Falcons are goal-oriented and fearless creatures. They embody authority and intelligence, representing freedom and victory.

Flamingo: Flamingos bring balance and clear-sightedness. They symbolize love, power, and happiness, reminding you of the importance of staying centered.

Fox: Foxes are quick-witted and lucky animals. They embody adaptability, curiosity, and cunning, bringing playfulness to their actions.

Frog: Frogs represent transformation, sensitivity, and rebirth. They represent fertility, cleansing, and peace, showcasing their inherent power.

G

Gazelle: Gazelles are alert and swift creatures. They bring consciousness, anticipation, and refinement, embodying a sense of lightness.

Goat: Goats symbolize firmness and self-reliance. They possess vigor and alertness, representing strength and independence.

Grasshopper: Grasshoppers bring good fortune and wealth. They embody innovation, vision, and dynamic progress, reflecting a sense of optimism.

Giraffe: Giraffes represent individuality and intelligence. They bring peace and farsightedness, often displaying cleverness and gentleness.

Goose: Geese embody joy, bravery, and guidance. They stand for fertility, loyalty, and teamwork, showcasing vigilance and wisdom.

Goldfinch: Goldfinches are courageous and dedicated creatures. They bring happiness, luck, and originality to their presence.

H

Hawk: Hawks symbolize vision and alertness. They embody nobility, cleansing, creative strength, and inspiring courage in their actions.

Hedgehog: Hedgehogs offer protection and flexibility. They possess patience, kindness, and self-dependence, showcasing strength in vulnerability.

Hippopotamus: Hippos embody strength, protection, and wisdom. They are hard-working and balanced creatures, symbolizing fertility in their actions.

Horse: Horses represent freedom, adventure, and endurance. They bring mobility and independence, reflecting friendship and the ability to overcome challenges.

Heron: Herons symbolize independence and balance. They bring a calm and intrusive nature, often multitasking with self-determination.

Hummingbird: Hummingbirds represent flexibility, love, and wisdom. Their small yet powerful presence embodies hope, healing, and aggression.

I

Inchworm: Inchworms symbolize logic, transformation, and subtlety. They bring a sense of concealment and transmutation in their actions.

J

Jellyfish: Jellyfish represent faith and transparency. They embody illumination, sensitivity, and protection, often with intentional movements.

Jaguar: Jaguars symbolize power, loyalty, and grace. They are known for their speed, knowledge, fertility, and rejuvenating energy.

K

Koala: Koalas embody gratitude and healing. They bring calmness, trust, empathy, and protection, often associated with a sense of magic.

Kiwi: Kiwis are alert and faithful creatures. They hold authority and cultural significance, showcasing genius and togetherness.

L

Ladybug: Ladybugs bring good luck, true love, and innocence. They represent metamorphosis and illusionary intervention, often linked to positive change.

Lion: Lions symbolize pride, courage, and power. They are natural-born leaders with authority, wisdom, and fiery energy.

Lizard: Lizards embody imagination, spirituality, and adaptability. They showcase quick-wittedness and intrusiveness, often linked to exploring the unknown.

Loon: Loons represent patience, calm, and connection. They bring faithfulness, satisfaction, and a sense of refreshment to their presence.

M

Magpie: Magpies embody flexibility and communication. They symbolize fate, love, and opportunity, often carrying an optimistic attitude.

Monkey: Monkeys are bold and confident creatures. They are compassionate and playful yet also aggressive and rebellious, reflecting a mix of qualities.

Moose: Moose represents endurance, intelligence, and strength. They embody dignity, femininity, and impulsiveness in their actions.

Mosquito: Mosquitoes symbolize persistence and agility. They possess direction and self-confidence, often acting as indicators of their surroundings.

Mouse: Mice symbolize stealth, modesty, and understanding. They are grounded creatures with an eye for detail and innocence in their actions.

Mockingbirds: Expressive and thankful, they bring defensive and lively energy. They encourage creativity and togetherness.

Meadowlark: They symbolize satisfaction and joy. A sense of arousal, modesty, and manifestation accompanies their wisdom.

O

Orangutan: These animals embody creativity and gentleness. They often seek solitude and possess ingenuity, honor, and logic.

Opossum: Opossums represent wisdom and sensibility. They are humble creatures that emphasize togetherness, extraordinary qualities, and decisiveness.

Otter: Otters are lively and cheerful animals that bring kindness and sensibility. Their dynamic nature is associated with happiness.

Ox: Oxen symbolizes sacrifice and monogamy. They are grounded creatures known for longevity, strength, and loyalty.

Osprey: Ospreys represent balance and vision. They embody potentiality and rigor, often seeking opportunities with precise timing.

Owl: Owls are known for wisdom and being secret keepers. They also symbolize freedom, comfort, stealth, vision, protection, and sometimes deception.

P

Panda: Pandas symbolize adaptability and balance. They represent determination, willpower, diplomacy, inner sight, and solitude.

Panther: Panthers represent courage, valor, and power. They are protective and can be both aggressive and feminine in their demeanor.

Peacock: Peacocks bring beauty and knowledge. They embody self-esteem, foresight, endurance, royalty, love, and sexuality.

Penguin: Penguins are community-minded and graceful creatures. They symbolize discipline, confidence, sacrifice, spirituality, and determination.

Pelican: Pelicans are strong and selfless animals. They bring warmth, responsibility, defensiveness, and kindness.

Porcupine: Porcupines symbolize innocence and vision. They tend to be self-involved and humble, seeking togetherness despite anxious tendencies.

R

Rabbit: Rabbits are creative and prosperous animals. They embody intensity, love, cleverness, sensitivity, harmony, and imagination.

Rat: Rats symbolize kindness and fertility. They possess foresight, intelligence, abundance, strength, success, and stealth.

Ram: Rams can be aloof and sensitive but also hard-working and visionary. They represent transformation and anxious tendencies.

Rhinoceros: Rhinos symbolize intelligence and isolation. They are decisive and enduring creatures, often possessing a liberated and insightful nature.

Raccoon: Raccoons represent confidentiality and illusion. They are brave and empathetic creatures known for versatility and protection.

Reindeer: Reindeer represents accomplishment and abundance. They embody endurance, strength, faith, tenacity, and protection.

Rooster: Roosters are fearless and unique. They bring intimacy, ego, nonconformity, and sometimes an intrusive quality.

S

Snake: Snakes can be impulsive and powerful. They symbolize shrewdness, transformation, magic, fear, wisdom, and healing.

Salmon: Salmon embody dignity and seriousness. They possess intelligence and the ability to experience a resurgence. They hold spiritual and firm qualities.

Swan: Swans are graceful and pure. They bring love, beauty, power, elegance, devotion, calmness, and balance.

Spider: Spiders symbolize patience and creativity. They offer protection, growth, aptitude, networking, balance, and wisdom.

Sheep: Sheep represents compassion and peace. They embody purity, courage, progress, level-headedness, and humility.

Squirrel: Squirrels are playful and social animals. They bring balance, passion, trust, hard work, and resourcefulness.

Stork: Storks symbolize resurgence and creativity. They represent responsibility, boldness, protection, and fertility.

T

Tiger: Tigers embody valor, power, and pride. They are devoted and fearless, symbolizing vigor, passion, and royalty.

Turtle: Turtles represent wisdom and patience. They possess speed, endurance, fertility, longevity, protection, and peace.

Turkey: Turkeys symbolize gratification and generosity. They emphasize connection, togetherness, hard work, and wealth.

Tarantula: Tarantulas symbolize creativity and patience. They are known for self-protection, transformation, and sometimes intimidation.

U

Unicorn: Unicorns symbolize magic and love. They embody faith, vision, innocence, purity, gentleness, and grace.

V

Vulture: Vultures bring loyalty, patience, and quick-wittedness. They are goal-oriented, trusting, and perceptive animals.

W

Wasp: Wasps are aggressive and creative creatures. They represent fertility, intelligence, teamwork, enthusiasm, and determination.

Wolf: Wolves symbolize protection and partnership. They bring loyalty, compassion, spirituality, togetherness, and power.

Whale: Whales represent wisdom, power, and strength. They embody self-reliance, protection, bravery, and a connection to ancestry.

Woodpecker: Woodpeckers symbolize intelligence and healing. They bring a unique perspective, connection, revelation, and perception.

Conclusion

Nature has a plan for everything, believe it or not. Even when things seem weird or animals act strangely, they're not just messing around, and it's not just a coincidence. There's actually a method to the madness. Think about it: do you always understand why people act the way they do? No, right? The same goes for the animals out there. Sometimes, you don't click with what you don't understand, and that's human nature. However, a deeper knowledge can actually help you drop those biases and misconceptions.

So, there's no need to label any animal as "bad" or "negative." In nature, there are no mistakes or missteps. Everything has its place, and there is a place for everything. It's only we humans who put labels on everything, often without understanding the whole picture.

Have you ever thought about animals from a mystical angle? Some people worry that they'll start imagining animals as little humans or gods. Sure, you might get a tad superstitious, but remember, most superstitions are not bad. The more you dive into the animal world and nature, the more you're going to believe in spiritualism, the unseen forces, and the universe's plan.

However, before you can start interpreting signs and messages from animals, you have to understand what message is being conveyed. This is where this book comes in. It shows you how every animal has its own uniqueness. Animals are these little reminders of how incredible you are, too. Each time you see an animal in a fresh light, you're basically finding something new and unique about yourself.

So, if you want to understand power animals and have them as your spiritual guides, you must keep an open mind when implementing all the teachings you've learned through this book. These pages were intended to serve as a gateway into the incredible influence of animals. Hopefully, you've learned something valuable from these teachings and will work to use them in your life. You'll be surprised to see the difference it makes to how you live!

Here's another book by Silvia Hill that you might like

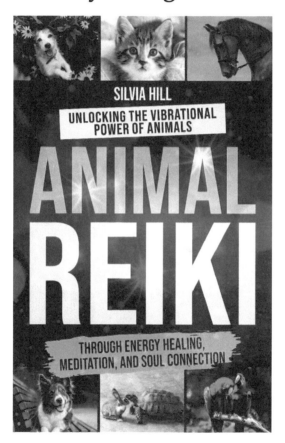

Free Bonus from Silvia Hill available for limited time

Hi Spirituality Lovers!

My name is Silvia Hill, and first off, I want to THANK YOU for reading my book.

Now you have a chance to join my exclusive spirituality email list so you can get the ebooks below for free as well as the potential to get more spirituality ebooks for free! Simply click the link below to join.

P.S. Remember that it's 100% free to join the list.

$27 FREE BONUSES

᭙ 9 Types of Spirit Guides and How to Connect to Them

᭙ How to Develop Your Intuition: 7 Secrets for Psychic Development and Tarot Reading

᭙ Tarot Reading Secrets for Love, Career, and General Messages

Access your free bonuses here
https://livetolearn.lpages.co/power-animals-paperback/

References

(N.d.). Masterclass.com. https://www.masterclass.com/articles/how-to-lucid-dream

(N.d.-a). A-z-animals.com. https://a-z-animals.com/blog/dreaming-of-elephants-discover-the-spiritual-meaning-and-interpretation/

(N.d.-b). A-z-animals.com. https://a-z-animals.com/blog/dreaming-of-wolves-discover-the-spiritual-meaning-and-interpretation/#:~:text=The%20wolf%20dream%20is%20a,a%20window%20into%20your%20character

[No title]. (n.d.). Samanthabritt.Co.Uk. https://samanthabritt.co.uk/Building_a_Medicine_Wheel.html

3 spirit animal meditations. (n.d.). Gaia. https://www.gaia.com/article/3-spirit-animal-meditations

3 spirit animal meditations. (n.d.). Gaia. https://www.gaia.com/article/3-spirit-animal-meditations

4 ways to meditate with a power animal - wikiHow health. (2012, October 23). Wikihow.Health; wikiHow. https://www.wikihow.health/Meditate-With-a-Power-Animal

Äikäs, T., & Fonneland, T. (2021). Animals in Saami shamanism: Power animals, symbols of art, and offerings. Religions, 12(4), 256. https://doi.org/10.3390/rel12040256

Äikäs, T., & Fonneland, T. (2021). Animals in Saami shamanism: Power animals, symbols of art, and offerings. Religions, 12(4), 256. https://doi.org/10.3390/rel12040256

Äikäs, T., & Fonneland, T. (2021). Animals in Saami shamanism: Power animals, symbols of art, and offerings. Religions, 12(4), 256. https://doi.org/10.3390/rel12040256

Aletheia. (2014, February 5). 7 ways to connect with your spirit animal. LonerWolf. https://lonerwolf.com/spirit-animal/

Ancient Egyptian gods and goddesses. (2014, August 27). Discovering Ancient Egypt. https://discoveringegypt.com/ancient-egyptian-gods-and-goddesses/

Andras, S. (2013, July 31). 20 amazing facts about dreams that you might not know about. Lifehack. https://www.lifehack.org/articles/productivity/20-amazing-facts-about-dreams-that-you-might-not-know-about.html

Animal powers in dreams. (2014, July 18). Keen.com; Keen. https://www.keen.com/articles/spiritual/animal-powers-in-dreams

Animal Totems. (n.d.). Universe of Symbolism. https://www.universeofsymbolism.com/animal-totems.html

Animals in Japanese Folklore. (n.d.). Nga.gov. https://www.nga.gov/features/life-of-animals-in-japanese-art.html

Arlin Cuncic, M. A. (2023, June 30). What it means when you dream about snakes, according to dream experts. Verywell Mind. https://www.verywellmind.com/what-does-it-mean-when-you-dream-about-snakes-7550333

Barkley, S. (2014, March 20). Do affirmations work? Research, psychology, and tips. Psych Central. https://psychcentral.com/health/why-positive-affirmations-dont-work

Basalt Spiritual. (2022, December 5). 13 spiritual meanings when you dream about A fox. Basalt Spiritual. https://www.basaltnapa.com/dream-about-a-fox/

Basics on sleep. (n.d.). WebMD. https://www.webmd.com/sleep-disorders/sleep-101

Bear in dreams - dream interpretation and meaning of bear in dreams. (n.d.). Cafeausoul.com. https://www.cafeausoul.com/oracles/dream-dictionary/bear

Bevan, K. (2023, January 23). The Shamanic Journey - Accessing The Invisible Worlds. The Daily Dish - Creative Vegan Recipes. https://dailydish.co.uk/the-shamanic-journey-accessing-the-invisible-worlds/

Campion, A. (2014, March 11). Animals in dreams: Shamans, Spirit Guides, and shapeshifters. The Dream Well. https://thedreamwell.com/animals-in-dreams-shamans-spirit-guides-and-shapeshifters/

Can anxiety cause a dream overload? (2020, October 10). Calmclinic.com. https://www.calmclinic.com/anxiety/symptoms/dream-overload

Capas, A. (2023, May 12). Sleep meditation: What it is, benefits and how to do it. Cleveland Clinic. https://health.clevelandclinic.org/sleep-meditation/

Carter, R. (2023, January 15). Animals in Norse mythology: A guide to Nordic animals. Scandification. https://scandification.com/animals-in-norse-mythology-nordic-animals/

Charles, A. (2022, April 6). How to Identify and work with your power animal. Spirituality+Health. https://www.spiritualityhealth.com/how-to-identify-and-work-with-your-power-animal

Charles, A. (2022, April 6). How to Identify and work with your power animal. Spirituality+Health. https://www.spiritualityhealth.com/how-to-identify-and-work-with-your-power-animal

Charles, A. (2022, April 6). How to Identify and work with your power animal. Spirituality+Health. https://www.spiritualityhealth.com/how-to-identify-and-work-with-your-power-animal

Childs, M. L. (2018, August 27). Anansi – deity or storybook trickster? Ancient Origins. https://www.ancient-origins.net/myths-legends-africa/anansi-0010612

Connecting with your power animal. (n.d.). Kripalu. https://kripalu.org/resources/connecting-your-power-animal

Desy, P. L. (n.d.). 4 Spirit Keepers of the Native American Medicine Wheel. Learn Religions. https://www.learnreligions.com/medicine-wheel-power-animals-1731122

Dolphin in dreams - dream interpretation and meaning of dolphin in dreams. (n.d.). Cafeausoul.com. https://www.cafeausoul.com/oracles/dream-dictionary/dolphin

Dream Dictionary. (n.d.). Cafeausoul.com. https://www.cafeausoul.com/oracles/dream-dictionary

Dreaming of cats? You're not alone. (2022, June 4). Bettersleep.com. https://www.bettersleep.com/blog/dreaming-of-cats-youre-not-alone/

Dreams, J. I. (2018, July 13). Ape & gorilla dream meaning. Journey Into Dreams. https://journeyintodreams.com/ape-dream-meaning/

Drerup, M., PsyD, & DBSM. (2022, August 18). Why do we dream? Cleveland Clinic. https://health.clevelandclinic.org/why-do-we-dream/

Elephant in dreams - dream interpretation and meaning of elephant in dreams. (n.d.). Cafeausoul.com. https://www.cafeausoul.com/oracles/dream-dictionary/elephant

Estrada, J. L. (2023, April 4). The science of visualization and its impact on dream recall. Dream Jorney. https://dreamjorney.com/science-of-visualization-and-dream-recall/

Exploring the benefits of deep breathing before sleep. (2021, July 19). The Global Classroom. https://www.theglobalclassroom.com/exploring-the-benefits-of-deep-breathing-before-sleep/

Forneret, A. (2022, November 22). Dreaming of butterflies meaning & symbolism. Alica Forneret. https://alicaforneret.com/dreaming-of-butterflies/

Forneret, A. (2023, February 6). Dream about bats meaning: Fear, change, power & more. Alica Forneret. https://alicaforneret.com/dream-about-bats/

Fox dream meaning. (n.d.). Auntyflo.com. https://www.auntyflo.com/dream-dictionary/fox

Fox in Dreams - Its meaning, and symbolism might surprise you! - What Is My Spirit Animal. (2017, May 20). What Is My Spirit Animal | Spirit, Totem, & Power Animals; What Is My Spirit Animal. https://whatismyspiritanimal.com/animal-dream-symbols-a-m/what-does-dream-about-fox-mean/

Freedman, S. (2018, December 13). This Sequence Will Help You Tap Into the Power of Your Intuition. Yoga Journal. https://www.yogajournal.com/practice/yoga-sequences/yoga-for-intuition-poses-to-boost-your-intuitive-powers/

Garve, R., Garve, M., Türp, J. C., Fobil, J. N., & Meyer, C. G. (2017). Scarification in sub-Saharan Africa: social skin, remedy, and medical import. Tropical Medicine & International Health: TM & IH, 22(6), 708–715. https://doi.org/10.1111/tmi.12878

Goldman, R., & Young, A. (n.d.). Affirmations: What they are and how to use them. Everydayhealth.com. https://www.everydayhealth.com/emotional-health/what-are-affirmations/

Guida Navarro, A. (2021). Ecology as Cosmology: Animal myths of Amazonia. In H. J. Mikkola (Ed.), Ecosystem and Biodiversity of Amazonia. IntechOpen.

Haekel, J. (2022). totemism. In Encyclopedia Britannica.

Harris, E. (2016, October 5). The ultimate guide to spirit animals, power animals & totems. Spirit Animal Info. https://www.spiritanimal.info/

Harris, E. (2016, October 5). Ultimate guide to spirit animals, power animals & totems. Spirit Animal Info. https://www.spiritanimal.info/

Helfer, F. (2019, March 4). A simple relaxation yoga routine for beginners. Yoga Rove. https://yogarove.com/relaxation-yoga-routine/

How to do progressive muscle relaxation for anxiety. (2019, April 17). Anxiety Canada. https://www.anxietycanada.com/articles/how-to-do-progressive-muscle-relaxation/

How to find your animal. (n.d.). Star Animal Sundays. https://staranimalsundays.com/pages/find-your-spirit-animal

How To Find Your Power Animal - guided meditation. (n.d.). Universe of Symbolism. https://www.universeofsymbolism.com/how-to-find-your-power-animal-denise-linn.html

How to find your spirit animal or totem guide. (n.d.). Gaia. https://www.gaia.com/article/find-your-spirit-animal-meanings

How to Use A Native American Medicine Wheel. (2011, November 4). Sacredhoopdrums. https://sacredhoopdrums.wordpress.com/2011/11/04/how-to-use-a-native-american-medicine-wheel/

Janzer, C. (2022, April 8). How to lucid dream. Sleep.com. https://www.sleep.com/sleep-health/how-to-lucid-dream

Jiang, F. (2021, July 20). 20 CommonestAnimalDreams+ meanings (Chinese theory). Chinahighlights.com; China Highlights. https://www.chinahighlights.com/travelguide/culture/dreaming-about-animals.htm

Johnson, C. (2023, February 5). Spirit vs. totem vs power animal - where is the difference? Centerspirited.com. https://centerspirited.com/animal-symbolism/spirit-vs-totem-vs-power-animal/

Johnson, V. (2021, July 31). How the Shamanic Medicine Wheel Works. Jesse. TV. https://jesse.tv/how-the-shamanic-medicine-wheel-works/

Joseph, B. (2020, May 24). What is an Indigenous Medicine Wheel? Ictinc.Ca. https://www.ictinc.ca/blog/what-is-an-indigenous-medicine-wheel

Karma and luck. (n.d.). Totems: What Are They and What Is Their Purpose. https://www.karmaandluck.com/blogs/news/totems-what-are-they-and-what-is-their-purpose

Kedia, S. (2020, March 22). Spirit animal list. TheMindFool - Perfect Medium for Self-Development & Mental Health. Explorer of Lifestyle Choices & Seeker of the Spiritual Journey; TheMindFool. https://themindfool.com/spirit-animal-list/

Kendra Cherry, M. (2008, June 4). Why do we dream? Verywell Mind. https://www.verywellmind.com/why-do-we-dream-top-dream-theories-2795931

Kendra Cherry, M. (2023, January 4). What Are Stress Dreams? Verywell Mind. https://www.verywellmind.com/stress-dreams-7090775

Khuong, V. V. (1631727034000). POWER ANIMALS ~ working w/ spirit animals through SHAMANIC journeying. Linkedin.com. https://www.linkedin.com/pulse/power-animals-working-w-spirit-through-shamanic-victoria-vives-khuong/

Lion in dreams - dream interpretation and meaning of lion in dreams. (n.d.). Cafeausoul.com. https://www.cafeausoul.com/oracles/dream-dictionary/lion

Llewellyn. (2009, November 13). Exercise: Finding your power animal. Llewellyn Worldwide. https://www.llewellyn.com/journal/article/2067

Lucid dreams. (n.d.). WebMD. https://www.webmd.com/sleep-disorders/lucid-dreams-overview

Mammillaria hahniaia, Old Lady Cactus Plant - 3.5 inch Pot (1 Plant). (n.d.).

marshadelamothe. (2023, June 13). Animal spirits and shamanic rituals: A comprehensive guide.

marshadelamothe. (2023, June 13). Connecting with your power animal.

McLean, J. (2020, March 2). Bull Jumping ceremony in Ethiopia on my Omo Valley photo tour —. JAYNE MCLEAN PHOTOGRAPHER. https://www.jaynemclean.com/blog/2020/bull-jumping-ceremony-banna-tribe

McNamara, P. (2016, September 5). Why are dreams such potent vehicles for the supernatural? Aeon; Aeon Magazine. https://aeon.co/essays/why-are-dreams-such-potent-vehicles-for-the-supernatural

Monahan, J. B. (2018, August 7). Working with Your Power Animal. Medium. https://medium.com/@jennifermonahan_28426/working-with-your-power-animal-a5d4cdf00e5a

Myth - Creation, Origins, Beliefs. (n.d.). In Encyclopedia Britannica.

Native American totem animals & their meanings – legends of America. (n.d.). Legendsofamerica.com. https://www.legendsofamerica.com/na-totems/

Obringer, L. A., & Jeffcoat, Y. (2021, October 15). How dreams work. HowStuffWorks. https://science.howstuffworks.com/life/inside-the-mind/human-brain/dream6.htm

Old lady cactus Care (Watering, Fertilize, Pruning, Propagation). (n.d.). PictureThis. https://www.picturethisai.com/care/Mammillaria_hahniana.html

Power animals. (2015, February 21). Shaman Links. https://www.shamanlinks.net/shaman-info/the-spirit-world/power-animals/

Practical Psychology. (2022, December 19). Dreams of monkeys meaning. Practical Psychology. https://practicalpie.com/dream-of-monkeys/

Ralls, E. (2023, June 25). Do birds dream of flying? Scientists say they now know the answer. Earth.com. https://www.earth.com/news/do-birds-dream-of-flying-scientists-say-they-now-know-the-answer/

Rangaves, D. (2023, July 26). Dreaming about tigers? Here's what it means. Yahoo News. https://news.yahoo.com/dreaming-tigers-means-192308988.html?guccounter=1&guce_referrer=aHR0cHM6Ly93d3cuZ29vZ2xlLmNvbS8&guce_referrer_sig=AQAAAH1ROz_TfxAP46gDICHYK8uXtWFPAej2hs48Wb_OC2Zwcy2jlYnlZD3VZd_ZRCnzTs12Mfr5w2M8h2SFiINBak00bWOPAoHVa6NTdeXodE5xlDTxYH7hY2ViqqXprgRiZTyA5XFSk_sMnKGnRthAO4Ic3OwChv_1f8XBbVVh4hwK

Raven, S. (2020, September 29). Wild dog. Spirit Animal Totems. https://www.spirit-animals.com/wild-dog-symbolism/

Relaxation techniques: Try these steps to reduce stress. (2022, April 28). Mayo Clinic. https://www.mayoclinic.org/healthy-lifestyle/stress-management/in-depth/relaxation-technique/art-20045368

Reptiles in dreams - dream interpretation and meaning of reptiles in dreams. (n.d.). Cafeausoul.com. https://www.cafeausoul.com/oracles/dream-dictionary/reptiles

Richardson, T. C. (2021, March 17). 6 Types Of Spirit Guides & How To Communicate With Them. Mindbodygreen. https://www.mindbodygreen.com/articles/types-of-spirit-guides

Sanz, E. (2022, February 23). Dream incubation: Dreaming with a purpose. Exploring Your Mind. https://exploringyourmind.com/dream-incubation-dreaming-with-a-purpose/

Shamanism & power animals – shamanism UK. (n.d.). Shamanismuk.com. https://www.shamanismuk.com/shamanism-power-animals/

Shamanism and dreams. (n.d.). Dream-institute.org. https://dream-institute.org/articles/shamanism-and-dreams/

Sophia. (2017, August 12). Does your subconscious mind control your dreams? The Wisdom Post. https://www.thewisdompost.com/law-of-attraction/subconscious-mind/does-your-subconscious-mind-control-your-dreams/1003

Sophia. (2017, August 12). Does your subconscious mind control your dreams? The Wisdom Post. https://www.thewisdompost.com/law-of-attraction/subconscious-mind/does-your-subconscious-mind-control-your-dreams/1003

Sophie. (2023, March 12). Unlock the spiritual meaning of your dreams with animal dream interpretation.

Spirit Animal vs Totem and Power Animal – Understanding the key differences. (n.d.). Crystallized Collective. https://crystallizedcollective.us/blogs/news/spirit-animal-vs-totem-and-power-animal-understanding-the-key-differences

Spirit Animals A-Z. (2021, November 23). Spirit Animals. https://www.spiritanimals.org/spirit-animals-a-z/

Stephen, D. B. (2014, March 18). Power Animal Retrieval. Bear With Me. https://drakebearstephen.wordpress.com/2014/03/18/power-animal-retrieval/

Stout, J. H. (n.d.). How to incubate dreams. Trans4mind.com. https://trans4mind.com/jamesharveystout/dream-4.htm

Suni, E. (2020, October 30). Dreams: Why we dream & how they affect sleep | sleep foundation. Sleep Foundation.

Sutton, J. (2021, December 20). 7 stress-relief breathing exercises for calming your mind. Positivepsychology.com. https://positivepsychology.com/breathing-exercises-for-stress-relief/

The Editors of Encyclopedia Britannica. (2023). Sekhmet. In Encyclopedia Britannica.

The Medicine Wheel. (2017, June 15). St. Joseph's Indian School. https://www.stjo.org/native-american-culture/native-american-beliefs/medicine-wheel/

The Seven Lessons of the Medicine Wheel. (n.d.). Saymag.Com. https://saymag.com/the-seven-lessons-of-the-medicine-wheel/

The Three Shamanic Worlds - by Roel Crabbé. (2019, July 30). RoelCrabbe.Com. https://www.roelcrabbe.com/articles-about-shamanism/the-three-shamanic-worlds/

The visualization definition and how it transforms your life. (n.d.). Betterhelp.com. https://www.betterhelp.com/advice/visualization/the-visualization-definition-and-how-it-transforms-your-life/

Thompson, L. (2016, June 28). You Asked: How do dreams work? Vital Record; Texas A&M Health Science Center. https://vitalrecord.tamhsc.edu/how-do-dreams-work/

Thorp, T. (2017, May 26). Everyday magic: 3 daily rituals to connect you to the present. Chopra. https://chopra.com/articles/everyday-magic-3-daily-rituals-to-connect-you-to-the-present

Took, N. (2021, October 6). Dream incubation – can you decide what to dream? The Sleep Matters Club. https://www.dreams.co.uk/sleep-matters-club/dream-incubation

Totem and Power Animals A -Z. (n.d.). Namaste. Co.Za. http://www.namaste.co.za/uploads/7/8/2/5/7825657/totem_candles-small.pdf

Totem animals and their meanings. (n.d.). Nativeamericanvault.com. https://www.nativeamericanvault.com/pages/totem-animals-and-their-meanings

Totems A-Z. (2020, December 16). All Totems. https://alltotems.com/animal-totems-a-z/

Trance. (n.d.). Mpg.De. https://www.cbs.mpg.de/249040/20150708-01

Tributsch, H. (2018). Shamanic trance journey with animal spirits: Ancient "scientific" strategy dealing with inverted otherworld. Advances in Anthropology, 08(03), 91–126. https://doi.org/10.4236/aa.2018.83006

Unicorn, M. (2023, June 23). Unicorn dreams meaning – interpret your dream! - UnicornYard 🦄 🐾. UnicornYard 🦄; Unicorn Yard. https://unicornyard.com/unicorn-dreams/

victoriaGB. (2023, May 5). 10 Simple Steps To Connect With Your Spirit Guides. Gabbybernstein.Com. https://gabbybernstein.com/spirit-guides/

View all posts by Gaia Love →. (2017, October 10). How To Meet Your Shamanic Power Animal Part One – Shamanism UK. Shamanismuk.Com. https://www.shamanismuk.com/meeting-shamanic-power-animal/

Vivid dreams: Causes of vivid dreams. (2022, June 9).

Warner, H. B. (2023, February 11). Unlock the meaning of animals in dreams to gain insight into your unconscious. Dreamin Sightful. https://dreaminsightful.com/animals-in-dreams/

What is a power animal? (2014, July 21). Dr. Steven Farmer. https://drstevenfarmer.com/what-is-a-power-animal/

What is a Spirit Animal? (2018, December 4). What Is My Spirit Animal | Spirit, Totem, & Power Animals; What Is My Spirit Animal. https://whatismyspiritanimal.com/animal-spirit-guides/what-is-a-spirit-animal-and-whats-the-difference-between-a-spirit-animal-vs-totem-vs-power-animal/

wikiHow. (2012, October 23). 4 Ways to Meditate With a Power Animal - wikiHow Health. Wikihow.Health; wikiHow. https://www.wikihow.health/Meditate-With-a-Power-Animal

wikiHow. (2012, October 23). 4 Ways to Meditate With a Power Animal - wikiHow Health. Wikihow.Health; wikiHow. https://www.wikihow.health/Meditate-With-a-Power-Animal

Wolf in dreams - dream interpretation and meaning of wolf in dreams. (n.d.). Cafeausoul.com. https://www.cafeausoul.com/oracles/dream-dictionary/wolf

Wolf. (n.d.). Auntyflo.com. https://www.auntyflo.com/dream-dictionary/wolf

Wright, K. W. (2023, April 7). Dream journal: Tips, prompts, and a template for dream journaling. Day One | Your Journal for Life; Day One Journal App. https://dayoneapp.com/blog/dream-journal

Made in United States
Troutdale, OR
04/29/2024

19524703R10086